T0149346

LIISA HALME

A
Crash Course
in
EMOTIONAL
FREEDOM

How to Turn Your
Biggest Life Challenges into Opportunities
for Healing and Transformation

BALBOA.
PRESS

A DIVISION OF HAY HOUSE

Balboa Press books may be ordered through booksellers or by contacting:

Balboa Press
A Division of Hay House
1663 Liberty Drive
Bloomington, IN 47403
www.balboapress.com.au
1 (877) 407-4847

Print information available on the last page.

ISBN: 978-1-5043-1895-2 (sc)
ISBN: 978-1-5043-2012-2 (hc)
ISBN: 978-1-5043-1896-9 (e)

Balboa Press rev. date: 04/07/2020

Contents

Part 3 – The mind stuff

To all my teachers, near and far. Thank you for opening my eyes.

Read this first

What does freedom really mean to you? Does it mean being able to do the things you love and waking up excited about life every day? Does it mean freedom from crippling anxiety, or the freedom to be yourself, express your thoughts and emotions without fear?

You can live in a free country, have a passport that enables you to travel where you like, you may have financial freedom and the means to live the lifestyle you desire. You may be free to choose whom to marry, what to believe in and what to do with your life. You can choose your career and path. But you can still be a prisoner to your own emotional pain, your defenses and unwanted patterns that run your life and determine what kind of relationships you end up in and what levels of success, health and happiness you allow yourself to have – totally unconsciously. You may *still* not be truly happy or free.

A classic yogic mantra goes: *'Lokah, samastah, sukhino bhavantu' – may all beings everywhere be happy and free*. This is my desire: to see all beings happy and free. It does not mean the absence of challenges or difficulties in life, or the absence of pain. They are all a part of this human existence and experience. But we *can* learn to be truly happy and free amongst them (far beyond the 'stiff upper lip' or the fake smile we put on for a show of a brave face when all we really want to do is scream).

I did *not* write this book to help you 'fix yourself', or even to help you become a 'better person'. In fact I live in a paradigm (personal reality) where there is absolutely nothing inherently wrong with you, or anyone; there never was and never will be. In my reality you were born lovable and divine, even if your current experience appears or feels contrary. Sometimes we forget that we are enough, and can live our lives in a reality of lack, hardship, stressful relationships, dissatisfaction and emotional struggle. I've been there too, and sometimes still pop in for a visit. But if you'd rather live in a different reality of fulfilling relationships, personal peace, connection, joy and abundance, then read on.

In order to shift those areas of your life that are not working for you, you need get to know yourself fully and get real about what it is that isn't working. Then you can, bit by bit, deconstruct the prison that you have unknowingly built for yourself. This book is written as a manual to help you on that journey and expand from your old reality into a new paradigm where you meet those long lost parts of yourself, learn to get to know, accept and even love them, and thus remember your worthiness, beyond what you could currently imagine. Because that's what you are: worthy of your heart's true desires. You are a divine being from a divine source full of spirit and potential, and so it is.

You may already agree with this on a mental level, but often we are riddled with strong unconscious beliefs that speak differently. If your physical reality (= home, job, health, wealth, relationships, etc.) does not match the conscious idea you have about your value, then you can be sure that contrary unconscious thoughts and beliefs are keeping you from fully embodying it and acting accordingly.

Now it is time to embrace all of life's experience and deepen intimacy with yourself and life itself, in all its messiness. These chapters and practical exercises will help you choose freedom wherever you feel stuck.

LET THE EXPLORATION BEGIN!

First of all we need to get clear about where we are *not* happy and free. There will be some necessary inventory of old piles of dirt – our old beliefs about ourselves and the world that no longer work for us; old defenses and masks that give us a false sense of safety, but deep down keep us feeling alone, misunderstood and unloved. We really need to 'let that shit go' before we can enter into our new reality, and, before we can *truly* and completely let it go, we need to fully *own* it. I mean really, really own it, down to the dirty, yukky detail.

This can be a challenging process, particularly the part where we become aware of the dysfunctional patterns, beliefs and hidden personalities that keep us stuck, but have not yet changed them. It is probably the most annoying part!

However, the good news is that bringing our unconscious motives and pay-offs into our conscious awareness will eventually help us shift them, with little effort. It is a process that goes well beyond just reading the book: it's an ongoing practice. I wrote this book for myself too. I also need to keep actively practicing the principles that I know work!

I promise you freedom

A word of warning: You may not like some of the content in this book! I am aware that some, or rather a lot, of this stuff is quite confronting. When you do get triggered by what you read – or anything in life for that matter – I recommend you go through that part again, extra carefully, as there will be something important for you. The moments when we get triggered are always prime opportunities for learning. They are where the treasure is hidden! Who said self-development was always going to be fun?! Well, when you are digging into some of the deepest corners of yourself it isn't always going to be pretty. But what I can guarantee is that it will be worth it. I promise it will be worth persisting through the momentary resistance and discomfort. I promise you freedom; nothing less.

What if you've already tried it all?

By my early thirties I had read about every self-development book under the sun, done dozens of courses and tried as many healing modalities. I was eating healthily, exercising, meditating, looking after myself, practicing and teaching yoga and doing all the 'right things', but something still wasn't working in my life. I kept having difficult relationships and some persistent health problems, and was in a lot of emotional pain. Then I came across emotional work, including breathwork, body psychotherapy and core energetics, all of which changed my life, health and relationships completely, from the inside out.

I realized that in order to become enlightened / enlighten ourselves we need to bring light into the darkness that is in us. In other words, to become conscious we need to bring that which is unconscious into the light of consciousness.

This is something we have grown very afraid to do; to explore our darkness. We are under the impression that by ignoring it and disowning it we make it disappear – or that by looking at it or exposing it we will make it grow. We are taught that by our positive affirmations and denial of our painful emotions and negative thoughts we turn into creatures of light. We concentrate on the positive and always try to see the upside, and we wonder why we stay stuck, why we still feel in so much pain. It must be the world, then. It must be the others, causing it…?

This is what is different and noteworthy here: I am saying that we have been given the wrong instructions, or perhaps we have misunderstood them. We need to turn toward our pain, not away from it. It actually is vital, crucial and inevitable that we must explore, deeply get to know, accept and even love our darkness; all of that which we are ashamed of and would rather hide away, in order to become unstuck and have the life we desire - that life of freedom that I speak of.

Of course we don't *have to* go there if we don't want to; the choice is ours. But we need to be aware that, the longer we avoid our blind spots or our shadow and ignore its existence, the longer and stronger it keeps running our lives!

This is where a lot of self-development and spiritual practice falls short

- It bypasses the deep emotional work, which means our unprocessed and unconscious emotions keep us stuck, and the progress is tediously slow.
- It teaches us methods of avoiding, numbing or overriding our pain rather than becoming closely intimate and comfortable with it.
- It pushes us to identify with a smaller and smaller part of ourselves (that which is forever positive, loving, forgiving, compassionate, healthy, happy, successful, fill in the blank) – leaving the remaining parts of us disowned, hidden and unconscious.

Eventually we may even start to believe that narrow identification is who we are, and become completely unconscious of all of the rest, which we judge as unacceptable. This is actually pretty dangerous, because it is those unconscious emotions and parts of ourselves that really drive us. When this happens we become more and more intolerant of other people and their darkness. We simply cannot bear to look at it. This makes love very, very difficult – almost impossible – and we wonder why our life just isn't working out the way we'd like it to!

When I was exposed to some of the concepts I share in this book, they triggered the hell out of me. I had spent my whole life gathering evidence and a story of another kind (you'll understand what I mean later as I share my experiences and my process) and then I was told to throw it all out the window and take responsibility for everything that happens in my life. What happened was I defended my old shitty story like my life depended on it. It was a crappy reality of betrayal, necessary defense, painful relationships and constant inner battle, and yet, on some level, I didn't want to let it go. I defended my right to make others wrong and remain a disempowered victim (even if I never would have admitted it). Think about it – that's insane!

But this is what we do. We hang onto our story – we hang onto our misery – even though it's not really working for us, because it is familiar. It is what we know and we believe it is the only reality. Of course it is real for us, but in truth it is only one of an infinite number of possible realities. So I am asking you to trust me as a friend, like I trusted my teachers when I was so desperate I had nothing to lose. It will require not just intellectual understanding of these principles, but embodying them in your daily life by constant practice.

HOW TO USE AND READ THIS BOOK

I have avoided too many words and tried to make the messages concise. No matter how short, each chapter is a big bite to swallow and may take some time for you to digest, put into practice and integrate. The chapters work as a whole and support each other. You may read them in any order, but they will make the most sense when read in the order in which they appear.

This is not a guide on how to live your life, or how to manage stress or anger or control your emotions, but on how to know yourself fully. It is not something I have come up with myself, but what I have been taught by various teachers in numerous different ways, then practiced and found effective. I have simply put it into my own words as I have experienced in my own life. There is no theory here that hasn't been tested over years and years by millions of people around the world in real life, in real relationships, careers, passions and real life challenges. I have used my own life and story in the many personal examples, and leave it up to you to apply the principles to your own life and experiences. Go ahead and fill in the blanks with your own emotions, situations and people in your life; swap *she* for *he* and so on.

The contents of this book can show you a way to true freedom, love, power and joy. Buckle up and dive in. Your life will never be the same again.

PART 1

Emotions: the dark side

Emotional literacy – emotions 101

We live with our emotions every day. Sometimes they take us higher than all the drugs on the planet, and other times cause us a lot of pain.

We are all emotional beings and emotions are an integral part of our life and existence, whether we are aware of them or not. But most of us weren't taught at home or at school how to recognize, process or express our emotions in a healthy way. In fact, the less aware of our emotions we are (the less 'emotional' we think we are), the more they influence us unconsciously. This is why it is helpful to understand and learn to read them; to become emotionally literate.

It is known that only about 10% or less of all our decision-making is influenced by the conscious, logical, rational mind (the neocortex part of the brain). Let's think for a moment what this means. Consider all those hundreds, even thousands, of decisions and choices about how we interpret or respond to things, our likes and dislikes, and how we live our life every single day.

Isn't it astonishing that the remaining 90% happens in the unconscious mind and the older parts of the brain that are linked to our emotions, instincts and intuition?

So the more in touch with our emotions we are on a day-to-day basis, the more aware we are of what really drives us.

As we become more in tune with our emotions we can make more conscious choices every day about how to live, how we respond or react to things, and how we interpret events and things around us. We begin to embrace all of life's experiences instead of running away from pain and seeking pleasure. We learn about ourselves, and through knowing ourselves better, we are able to be more authentic and have deeper connection with other people.

What is emotion?

Science now tells us what the yogis and mystics have known for thousands of years: everything is energy. Our emotions are different energies in the body-mind:

$$E\text{-motion} = \text{energy in motion}$$

Going with the flow

All energy needs to move. It can work for or against us – or, more accurately, we can work with it or against it: go with the flow or against the flow. It is never the emotion itself that causes problems. Energy is neutral; it is neither good nor bad.

We may have learnt to think of certain emotions as negative, something to be avoided, but in reality all emotions have their purpose. It's just that we don't know how to express them in a healthy way.

In the quest to be happy and free it is vital to learn to understand ourselves, to recognize and comprehend our so-called 'negative' (or more painful) emotions such as fear, anger, sadness, shame and guilt, as well as their healthy aspects.

So where do we begin? How do we become more emotionally literate? A good place to start is learning to recognize and name our emotions.

Sometimes we just feel something, and we can tell it is driving our actions, but we don't seem to be able to make much sense of it.

HERE IS THE 'EMOTIONAL ABC' MADE EASY

Anger is about power or control

This could be real or perceived loss of power; either giving it away – for example saying yes when we want to say no – or having our power taken away; being controlled by someone.

It's important to mention that even though anger is often equated with aggression or hostility, they are not the same thing. Aggression and hostility are something (toxic) we may *do* with anger.

Anger often pairs up with

- It's unfair
- I was wronged
- I deserved better

Expressions of anger include

- annoyance
- frustration
- resentment
- blaming
- making others wrong
- making others small in your mind
- having angry conversations in your head

Healthy anger gives us the courage and power to stop being helpless victims. It calls us to stand up for ourselves, for someone else or something we believe in. It helps us to be in our power, set healthy boundaries and take action. Healthy anger is connected to the heart and cares about the other. It is powerful, passionate and non-aggressive.

Grief / sadness has to do with love or loss

This could be real or perceived loss of love, for example, feeling:

- unsupported
- unloved
- neglected
- lonely
- rejected

Expressions of grief or sadness include

- melancholy
- apathy
- lack of enthusiasm
- tiredness
- dullness
- heavy or sluggish feeling in the body

Healthy grief is heart opening, cleansing and healing.

Fear is about safety or survival

This could be real or perceived danger or lack of safety.

Expressions of fear include

- anxiety
- stress
- nervousness
- dissociation
- hyper vigilance

- over analyzing
- controlling behavior
- OCDs
- restlessness
- difficulty to trust

Healthy fear keeps us from exposing ourselves or anyone else to real life- or health-threatening danger. It also stops us from risking things we aren't prepared to lose. For example 'they say this is a good investment. But if it goes wrong I could lose everything, including my house. I'm not prepared to take that risk.'

Shame is the feeling that 'there is something wrong with me', or feeling exposed in a painful way. Shame says 'I am not enough'.

In shame we can feel
- humiliated
- worthless
- ridiculed
- like we want to disappear or sink through the floor
- paralysed
- embarrassed

Shame of who we are or our humanity and imperfection can sometimes be covered up by perfectionism or acting superior (so that no-one will notice there is 'something wrong with us'; to cover up an inferiority complex).

Healthy versions of shame include humility or modesty. Healthy shame is usually felt about our actions (rather than who we are) and can urge us take responsibility and make better choices in the future. For example 'I'm ashamed of the way I acted. I'd had too much to drink and I said things that were not mine to share. I'm so sorry. I won't do that again!'

Guilt is the feeling that 'I have done something wrong'

Expressions of guilt could include frequent apologizing or feeling bad, sorry or apologetic for no good reason. Unhealthy guilt can make us beat ourselves up, or feel responsible for things that are out of our control. For example 'I feel guilty for having nice things when there are people in the world who have so little.'

A healthy version of guilt is wanting to make amends or apologize when we have acted out of integrity or hurt someone. A healthy version of guilt is also called a conscience. Similarly to healthy shame, healthy guilt leads to taking responsibility for our actions. For example 'I'm going to tell my boss it was me. He would never find out, but I just can't take the guilt. I can't let someone else lose their job because of what I did.'

Get to the core

To complicate things, our emotions often exist in layers: one or many emotions can be layered on top of another protecting the innermost core emotion. For example, when we are hurt by someone we may first feel anger and make the other person wrong as a defense not to feel the deeper pain.

In this case anger is a protective layer that keeps us from feeling the more vulnerable emotions of grief and sadness, of feeling unloved, rejected or abandoned.

We all have one emotion that we, when under stress, feel and express more easily than the others. It protects other emotions underneath it. When we get caught in the surface layers of our emotional experience we often stay stuck for longer than necessary, unable to move forward until we dive through into the deeper underlying emotions.

Through uncovering, owning and actually feeling the core emotion we can release the energy (emotion), process and perhaps communicate it in a conscious way, feel a shift in the situation, and move through it much more quickly.

PRACTICE TO IDENTIFY THE CORE EMOTION

Pick a recent situation that triggered something in you, or something that you reacted to.

Close your eyes, take a deep relaxed breath in, and then let it all out. Repeat this a couple more times. Let your inner awareness drop into your body. Notice where you feel the emotion in your body. Is it in the chest, the stomach, throat, or somewhere else?

Then ask yourself: is this about love or loss, about power or control, or about safety or survival? Just trust that you know the answer even if it's not obvious at first.

Use the 'emotional ABC' above to determine the core emotion. Even if you are not feeling the core emotion right now (as you may be feeling a surface emotion), know that it is the one you need to eventually get to in order to process the underlying energy in your body. Often just understanding this consciously can help you get in touch with the innermost and more vulnerable core emotion.

Give yourself permission to go there and feel it. Don't worry if it doesn't happen straight away; just allow yourself to keep connecting to the emotion until you feel it being released.

The difference between feelings and emotions

Feelings and emotions are inter-related but slightly different. You could say they are the two sides of the same coin.

Simply said, emotions are physiological and can be measured by blood flow, brain activity, facial expressions, body language and so on. Emotions are shared by all humans, even animals, even though we can be mentally unaware of them.

Feelings, on the other hand, are physical and mental sensations and cognitive reactions to the emotions. They are what you make of the emotions in your mind. Feelings are influenced by your personal experiences, associations and temperament. They are difficult to measure objectively and are individual to each person.

Urges and impulses sometimes get mistaken for feelings. 'I feel like a tub of double chocolate icecream' isn't actually a feeling. It's more of a desire.

Can't we just keep the 'good' and throw away the 'bad'?

When the heavier emotional energies aren't moving freely through the system they block the flow of joy, love, peace and other lighter energy frequencies as well. Once we get in touch with the deeper, more painful, difficult emotions we have perhaps tried to avoid, we'll soon find ourselves feeling more pure joy, peace and love as well.

Eventually we become familiar and comfortable with the full range of our inner experience, and start letting go of the judgments we have had about our painful or messy emotions.

Once we have released the excess internal pressure of the old stagnant energies and keep letting our emotions flow naturally, they will come, go and change like the weather without staying stuck or becoming toxic. We will simply enjoy them as the different flavors and colors of our life and experience!

When awareness is brought to an emotion, power is brought to your life.[1]
Tara Meyer Robson

From suppressing to owning our emotions

'What we resist persists' is an astute saying that certainly is true with our emotions. The emotions we don't want to feel – let alone own – stick around and influence us unconsciously.

Most of us weren't encouraged to openly express our 'negative' emotions while growing up. Maybe we were told it's unacceptable to be angry, or not to be a baby when we cried, or called silly when we were scared. Perhaps we had someone in our family circle who expressed their anger in a toxic, aggressive way and we decided never to be like that. Maybe it simply wasn't safe to express our feelings as we had to adapt to those of our caregivers.

It can be less socially acceptable for a girl to express anger than it is for a boy. On the other hand boys are commonly less encouraged to express sadness and fear, along the lines of: 'Don't be a girl' or 'Big boys don't cry'.

Our Western society also tells us to rely mainly on our intellect and rational thinking, and we often learn to think of emotions as something less important, weak or even stupid.

What's your emotional conditioning?

Do you make yourself or others wrong for certain emotions, or for being emotional?

Do you believe some emotions are acceptable but others are not?

Do you believe all or certain emotions are only acceptable and valid if they have a good reason or justification?

Do you sometimes think: 'I shouldn't be feeling like this.'?

Do you think you just aren't a very emotional person?

If so (and this goes for most of us), you could be suppressing some of your emotions.

Irrational emotions

It is common to use rationalizing as a way of suppressing our emotions. Unfortunately it doesn't make them go away – just works as a defense against feeling them. But here's the thing: emotions simply aren't logical. They originate from a completely different, older part of our brain and body-mind that has nothing to do with logic or reason but is more connected to our instincts and intuition.

This is why emotions often don't make much sense. They have nothing to do with our intellect or rational mind, yet they are an incredible resource of energy, personal power, and inner knowing.

Talking isn't always enough when dealing with emotional issues or trauma. By merely speaking about them on a conscious, rational level, we can understand them better, but it isn't enough to release them from the emotional and physical body. Hence we can be left with little or no relief.

The releasing happens through actually allowing ourselves to *feel* the emotions in our body and allowing them to be expressed through tears, sounds, different spontaneous breathing patterns, sweating, shaking or other natural ways in which the body releases emotional charge.

Think of a child having an emotional response and how their body expresses it, and how quickly it passes!

The crazy thing is that we can suppress our joy, love and other lighter emotions as well. We may have been told that expressing our childlike joy freely and loudly isn't okay, or maybe we learnt that there is something bad, wrong or sinful about pleasure, or that it isn't safe to love or receive love. We can be scared to feel happy in the fear that the pain will be too great when it all falls apart.

We also cannot suppress emotions selectively: When we suppress one, we suppress all. When we do our best to block out or hide our pain, we also block our joy, love and other lighter emotions.

When emotions become toxic

But does this mean that we should be venting our raw, intense, messy emotions at anybody, anytime without a filter? All of us have seen first hand that when emotion is expressed (or exploded) in a toxic way, it's both harmful and unhealthy. The difference is what we *do* with the emotions we have. Just because we feel something doesn't mean we have to *act on it.* It's the feeling part that we can't skip.

Paradoxically, suppressing tends to make emotions toxic
Problems usually start when we resist our emotions, make them wrong, deny them and hide them from ourselves and others. When we sit on unexpressed emotional content it eventually becomes unconscious and shows up in various messed up ways.

How do we *know* if we are carrying around disowned emotions?

Here are some indicators:

You get triggered by a particular emotion in others

Everyone tends to dislike and judge the emotion in other people that they don't want to own in themselves. So if your mum's fear and worrying really triggers you, it's possible you have some hidden fear of your own to get in touch with.

You see it everywhere

If you notice lots of anger or angry people everywhere, attract it into your life, often being the object of their anger, chances are that you have some anger to own yourself that keeps being reflected back to you through those around you! Once you begin to own your own anger, it will stop triggering anger in others, nor will you attract anger into your orbit in the same way.

The filters

If you seem to find sadness and misery everywhere you look, it is possible you are seeing the world through a filter of your own sadness. Accumulation of fear in the system, for example, can make the world seem a scary place full of danger, risks and lack of safety.

Blaming others

If you always find an outside reason or cause for your feelings ('I feel like this because he did that' or 'He made me feel like this') you are blaming others and avoiding taking ownership of how you feel. Almost everyone does this! It's good to remember that nobody can *make you* feel anything.

Recurring patterns in life

If you keep experiencing similar unwanted scenarios in your life, or situations in your relationships or your career that leave you feeling the same way, it could be because of disowned emotions. The pattern will keep repeating until you uncover, own and clear the underlying emotional cause.

Avoidance

When upset or hurt, if your tendency is to immediately do something in order not to feel it – keep busy, have a drink or a cigarette, over eat, over exercise, spend money on things you don't need, go out and be social – you could be avoiding your feelings. You can avoid facing challenging emotions by simply pretending they aren't there ('I'm not angry!'), or dodging talking about them with those involved. Even spiritual practices such as meditation can be (mis)used to numb out and avoid dealing with emotional pain.

You may also avoid your pain by telling yourself (and others) positive sounding lies designed to make you feel better and make things look fine on the outside, along the lines of 'I was getting sick of her anyway. I'm glad she broke it off.' However when engaging in the above avoidance tactics, you merely postpone the feeling and let it linger and affect you much longer than necessary.

The difference between *positive coping* and avoidance is that when using healthy coping tactics we still honor our emotions. We may go to a movie with a friend to cheer ourselves up when feeling down, but not to dismiss or escape how we feel. We may be able to see the silver lining in a situation whilst feeling our grief and accepting how we feel. When we avoid we don't give our emotions airtime, but deny or ignore the part of us that's in pain.

Emotional pressure cooker

When not expressed or released, emotional energy builds up and accumulates. This creates internal pressure in the physical and emotional body, which takes up more and more energy to keep it contained.

When the pressure gets too high for the body and our nervous system to hold, the built-up emotions explode at unexpected times in unexpected ways at people who have little or nothing to do with their origin – or they seep out sideways in less direct but equally destructive ways.

Even if we think we are doing a good job concealing how we feel, others can easily sense the vibe. Our emotions always get expressed, one way or another!

If our stuck emotional energies don't find a way out, the only other way for them to go is to turn inward. Scientists have actually found and identified the 'molecules of emotion'[2] showing how they get stored in the physical body and cellular memory. Over time they create negative feedback loops in the nervous system which can lead to physical pain and illness, anxiety, depression and other undesirable conditions.

On a mental level we might come up with unconscious negative beliefs about the world or ourselves that affect our happiness, relationships and everything we do.

Physiologically speaking we learn to literally swallow our emotions down and hold them in by tensing our muscles and restricting our breathing. This means less blood flow, and less oxygen available in the body. As a result other body functions such as digestion and metabolism are also affected. Over time we start to experience physical pain and eventually disease in those areas of the body.

Insufficient oxygen = all body functions suffer

These suppressed emotions (that we are often unaware of) also have a negative impact on our relationships, how we feel, and how we perceive and interpret the world.

The worse we feel, the less we breathe

An Australian PhD study by Lloyd Lalande[3] shows the correlation between neurotransmitter balance and breathing. Neurotransmitter imbalance in the long term leads to anxiety, brain fog, chronic pain, chronic fatigue, depression, and other health issues. The worse we feel, the less we breathe, which means even less oxygen and less optimal neurotransmitter production – and the vicious cycle is ready.

A simple breathwork practice has proven to be an effective, all-natural solution to reverse this cycle. It is no coincidence that, besides bringing more oxygen into the body, deep breathing also helps us release and shift stagnant emotional energies.

Energetically speaking

Holding or restricting breathing and tensing muscles stops energy (prana / chi / qi / ki) flow in that part of the body. As we swallow our emotional energy and accumulate it in the body, it creates energetic blockages and stagnation.

This could manifest in our life as feeling stuck, feeling like we don't have a choice, recurring negative patterns or chronic moods or physical pain that we can't seem to be able to shift.

Owning your emotions

Becoming aware of your unconscious emotions, owning them and feeling them paradoxically frees you from being controlled by them. It is also a significant step in loving and accepting yourself more fully: a key element to happiness!

A SIMPLE PRACTICE FOR OWNING YOUR FEELINGS

Each time you complain, vent or think over and over about something that happened, what someone said or did, some injustice, worry, annoyance or heartbreak, instead of getting caught up in the story (who said or did what), take it back to yourself and ask: *'How has this left me feeling?'* Try to keep the answer very short. (Long answers are likely to be just more of the story.)

The deeper answers will usually be a single word, such as,
It left me feeling:

- unloved
- unimportant
- angry
- scared
- ashamed
- embarrassed
- made wrong
- judged
- misunderstood

Drop your awareness down from your head and your thoughts and into your body. Notice your breath and make sure not to hold it. Stay with the feeling and allow it to be there. Then identify the accompanying emotion (fear / anger / sadness / shame / guilt). Tell yourself it's okay to feel it. This may mean it initially gets stronger as the emotion is being processed and released, but you'll notice it passing much more quickly.

Resist starting to think about the *story*: who did or said what, and what you interpret it to *mean*. The meaning we give it could be 'He doesn't love me'. Notice how this is different from 'I feel unloved.'

What's the story?

To summarize, the story is all stuff around the 'Thing' that happened (or didn't happen), the who said or did what, the whats, the hows and the whys. It is also about your interpretation about the event – what you make it mean in your head. For example, 'This proves he / she doesn't love / care about me'.

This story can be very real in your mind. However your truth may be completely different from the other party's truth. The story is always subject to interpretation. Your actual reality, once you drop the story, is the event that happened (without any interpretation) and how you are left feeling.

Expressing your feelings to others

As you get in the habit of doing this simple but powerful practice of owning your feelings and emotions, you are invited to do the same and use the same words when communicating with others. Simply stating how you feel is non-threatening and doesn't make the other person wrong. This leaves them nothing to defend against and creates an opening for them to be vulnerable as well.

This is the beautiful open-hearted space where real heart-to-heart connection can take place.

Remember that when you don't communicate your emotions directly, they will be expressed in some other sneaky and often much more destructive way! So, especially in intimate and close relationships, it's always worth communicating your challenging emotions, no matter how small or big, in the name of creating more intimacy and not sitting on things that create distance between you and your loved ones.

Owning your emotions sets you free as you realize they are not at the mercy of factors outside of yourself. It's a practice that will benefit you for the rest of your life. It will open your heart, reclaim your power and transform your relationships!

Liisa Halme

Understand your emotional triggers

Getting triggered (annoyed, frustrated, upset, defensive, anxious – you get the gist) affects how we feel, act and relate. In a triggered state it is difficult to be conscious or act reasonably; hence recurring triggers tend to have a negative impact on our relationships.

What's a trigger?

It could be someone or something that just presses your buttons or makes you react; that thing about a family member or a partner that always drives you crazy, or maybe a situation at work that you frequently complain about. Whatever the trigger, you'd probably rather live without the effect it has!

In the first thirty-something years of my life I used to get triggered several times a day. As a child it all tended to burst out without a filter (in fact I was the emotional valve for most of my core family), but then later on I learnt to suppress and hide it under clever disguises even from myself.

Even though I wasn't showing it on the outside, I was still getting triggered on the inside. Silently I would then make others wrong or make myself better-than, have imaginary conversations in my head, feel attacked or criticized, even when that wasn't actually the case, shut myself off, pretend not to be hurt when I was… All of this grew the gap between myself and others, and made authentic connection very hard.

One of the worst things about triggers is that a lot of the time our reaction is out of proportion with what has just happened. It doesn't necessarily seem that way at the time, but in hindsight, or in the eyes of others, it often is.

Out of proportion reactions

About 95% of the time (I made up this percentage, but you get the point) when we get triggered, our reaction has little or nothing to do with what has just happened. What has been triggered within us is a reaction to an old event (or events); an unresolved emotion or trauma. Many of these triggers reoccur many times over our lifetime, which means years worth of accumulated emotional charge comes to the surface at once. No wonder our reactions can sometimes seem out of proportion!

When we are triggered by someone or something – a situation in present life – it is usually a case of one of three things:

1. Reenactment or recreation of a past wound

Example: I was almost always the last kid to be picked up from daycare, and even though I put on a brave face, deep inside I felt abandoned, unloved and unimportant. Thirty years later when my husband arrives to dinner an hour late, my old childhood feelings of abandonment are triggered.

An event that seems small to someone else can feel big and significant to us: I feel unloved and unimportant, just like I did when I was a kid. In *his* reality he just had something unexpected going on at work that took all day, and then some.

Modern psychology and neuroscience teach that our brain gets wired in an individual way from a very early age, during which our sense of security and confidence, and our ability to love, bond and deal with challenges and stress, amongst many other important things, are learnt and embedded into our body-mind. Luckily, thanks to neuroplasticity, we have the ability to reprogram later on in life!

If I, for example, regularly experienced (real or perceived) abandonment in childhood I will be likely to recreate scenarios or feelings of abandonment in my relationships and interpret events through that specific filter.

I am familiar with the feeling, it is part of my reality and paradigm; so I keep re-creating and attracting it again and again, until I heal the original wound and clear the emotions and beliefs around it.

The recurring patterns in our life or relationships are often a case of re-creation of an old family dynamic involving Mum / Dad / other caregiver / sibling. For example, statistics show that people who have experienced regular abuse in childhood find themselves in abusive relationships again in adulthood significantly more often than those who had no experience of abuse in childhood.

2. *Projection*

This one is a classic – we project onto other people things that we don't want to admit about ourselves:

- She is so full of herself / pretentious / superficial
- What a control freak

- God, he is so needy it drives me crazy
- How can people be so unconscious!?!

Often a projection is a judgment we have about somebody else. When we begin to own these qualities or behavior in ourselves, they stop annoying us in others!

In relationships we have a tendency to look for the things we aren't giving ourselves. So, if I am unable to love and accept myself as I am, I will be looking for that missing love and acceptance outside of myself, getting triggered by its real or perceived absence.

Or if I am overly critical of myself I will be very sensitive to criticism from others (read: it will trigger me) and I will perceive criticism from others even when it's not there.

Another common example of a projection is when we believe we know what people think about us. We may believe they think we are stuck up, superficial, a loser, wrong…whatever judgment we have of ourselves, unconsciously. But most of us really aren't mind readers. Most often these judgments come from our very own subconscious mind – nowhere else!

3.   Disowned part of self

You may judge or dislike qualities in others that you *don't allow yourself to have*; those you have disowned.

Let's say you are an obsessive neat freak so you get triggered by people who are more relaxed about their surroundings or appearance.

If you have blocked off your emotions and rely only on your intellect, you may judge or make wrong people who are in touch with their feelings and express them freely. Or you may judge and make wrong people who are very successful or make lots of money doing what they love, because for some reason you haven't let yourself have that.

Even when we know *it's us, and not them,* it doesn't necessarily make us any less triggered. Even if we don't show it on the outside, triggers still affect us on the inside, and most likely will seep out some way through the tone of our voice or just through our energy. Hiding or internalizing our triggers doesn't make them go away. Quite the contrary, actually.

DAILY PRACTICE: HOW TO USE TRIGGERS IN YOUR FAVOR

Whenever you are triggered by or have a negative reaction to a situation or person or anything in life, try the following process.

Close your eyes, take a few deep, relaxed breaths, drop into your body. Ask yourself:

- Where do I feel it in my body?
- What does it feel like physically? (Does it feel contracted, tense, tight, hard, prickly, numb, cold, hot, piercing…? As much as possible, drop the story around it.)
- What's the emotion – anger, sadness, fear, shame or guilt? Then check if there is another emotion there. Often the first emotion we feel is a surface layer or a defense, and deeper core emotion will be hiding underneath. Naming our emotions goes a long way towards dissipating their charge.
- Is it a re-creation, a projection, or a disowned part of me?
- What can I relate it to in my childhood?
- Who does it remind me of: Mum, Dad, sibling / other?

So each time you get triggered, instead of making yourself (or others) wrong about it, remember it is a golden opportunity to learn about yourself and to release old patterns and feelings. This takes both humility and humor!

As a result you will get triggered less and less often, and when you do, it will pass much more quickly. When required you will be able to take more proactive action than you would in a reactive state. This will make your relationships and life in general a whole lot easier and more enjoyable.

Everything that irritates us about others can lead us to an understanding of ourselves.[4]
Carl Jung

What is really making us unhappy?

– from internal resistance to welcoming what is

It's probably safe to say that consciously we all have the desire to be happy. But we also know that life has its ups and downs and there will always be new challenges. So how do we retain our inner happiness or contentment amongst all of it?

I used to have this illusion that happiness meant the absence of so-called negative emotions: fear anger, sadness, shame or guilt. Even though I quite effectively suppressed and denied most of the above, I still wasn't as happy as I pretended to be. It wasn't working.

Through deep emotional work I discovered something surprising: true happiness was about welcoming and embracing all of our experience, including the pain and the chaos!

One of the major sources of our unhappiness is resistance to *what is*.

What is consists of our current circumstance, our experience of it and our emotions around it. When we are unhappy we are always resisting something. Often it is the heavier emotions like sadness, anger or fear. We make ourselves wrong for having them.

Sometimes we even resist feeling joy, pleasure or other light emotions too. Maybe we were frequently told off or yelled at when we were shrieking out of joy as a child, or we learnt to associate pleasure with something bad or naughty.

We may hold back from being happy out of a fear that it will be taken away and we'll be disappointed and feel even worse.

We resist certain things, like pain, partly just to avoid the pain itself, but also because we fear that by accepting them we give in, and give power to that which we don't want in our life. But the opposite is true: *resistance keeps us in an energetic bind; whereas acceptance releases it.*

The art of allowing

Acceptance is not the same as giving up or giving in. We also don't need to dissociate ourselves from what is happening around us. We can still stand up for ourselves, take action towards what we desire, set healthy boundaries, speak our truth and be in our power. In fact acceptance is very, very powerful.

When we begin to welcome whatever is there – the circumstance, our experience and our candid emotions around it – we free ourselves to be content again.

For example, when feeling deep grief, if we welcome it and allow that emotion to fully flow without resisting it, allowing our body to express it to its full extent, we will find a very sweet, healing quality in that expression.

Even if we feel sad we will be okay with the sadness, allowing it to be there. It will be just emotional energy moving through us like a waterfall, washing away stagnation and opening us for new energies that follow.

Giving yourself permission to feel the full extent of all your emotions and your experience is one of the keys to happiness. When you allow yourself to experience all emotions this way – authentically, fully and without resistance – they flow through and pass much more quickly, adding different flavors to life without binding you or keeping you stuck.

External circumstance vs. inner experience

It is always easy to find reasons outside of ourselves as to why we aren't happy, but each time we blame it on something external we give our power away and remain a victim to the circumstance.

I am not suggesting that you should blame yourself instead. Rather, you can take responsibility for your experience, and in doing so reclaim your power. Responsibility implies a choice. Suddenly you become the driver, not the driven.

The filters

It may seem as though we don't have a choice as to how we respond or react internally. However when we move from solely looking at external factors to investigating our inner reality and working with that, we'll find that we have much more choice than we think! Even if we are not able to change the circumstance, what we make of it is up to us.

Nothing and nobody can *make us* feel anything. The way we feel is our internal response, even if it is to an external event. Often our individual realities – our experience, interpretations and emotions – are very different, even contradictory, in exactly the same situation. They are just as real; only different.

It's like we are all wearing different glasses that we see the world through. The glasses filter what we see and affect how we perceive and respond to it. Becoming aware of our individual filter opens the opportunity to change it to one that serves us better, or to see right through it.

It's not personal

The more aware of our filters we are, the more we see through them, and the less personally we take life's events. We become aware that whatever we make events or other people's actions mean in our head is most often just our own interpretation, and may have nothing to do with their reality.

In short, it is usually my interpretation – what I make it mean – and my resistance to it that created the unhappiness; not the thing that happened.

This, however, does not mean that we ought to approach our intimate relationships, or the feelings of people close to us, with dissociated detachment, even though it is sometimes portrayed as some kind of spiritual higher ground. In reality it is just another way of avoiding feeling and avoiding intimacy. Some things *are* personal and need to be dealt with as such!

I also want to make clear that we have all the right in the world to turn pain into suffering or be unhappy; there is nothing wrong with that. Even simply welcoming our struggle or unhappiness we are already halfway there.

DAILY PRACTICE 1: WATERING THE GARDEN

Look for reasons to be unhappy and you'll find them. Likewise if you look for reasons to be happy, you will find them too. It is like watering your garden: the areas you water the most and give the most attention to will grow. If you water the flowers they will flourish. If you give all your attention to the weeds and water them, they will take over. It is your choice what you feed and grow in your garden.

DAILY PRACTICE 2: WELCOMING WHAT IS

When feeling unhappy or resistant about something, take a moment to just be, sit still, breathe, relax and ask yourself:

- Could I just welcome this situation?
- Could I just welcome my story around it; that which I make it mean?
- Could I just welcome my feelings around it?

If you feel resistance to the things above, ask:
- Could I just welcome my resistance to this?

You can change the word 'could' to 'would' and see if that makes a difference. Do a few rounds or until you get genuine positive answers. Notice how you feel in your body. Repeat again until you find yourself relaxing and feeling more at ease.

God grant me the serenity to accept the things
I cannot change, courage to change the things I can,
and wisdom to know the difference.[5]
Serenity Prayer by Reinhold Niebuhr

From victimhood to personal responsibility and freedom

Victimhood is not a particularly sexy topic, I know. Unless it is to do with war, major natural disasters, gruesome abuse or intended harm, tragic disease or other such gross misfortunes, the V-word is not one we like being associated with. Yet owning our inner victim is one of the biggest steps we can take towards true personal freedom.

Revealing questions

- Do you think the problems in your relationship are because of your partner, who really ought to change?

- Do you think you would be happier if only you had:
  - a better job
  - more money
  - a healthier or more beautiful body
  - an intimate relationship
  - more fun or conscious friends

  or if you could:
  - live somewhere else
  - do something else?

- Are you sure that there are external circumstances holding you back from living the life you want, or being who or where you want to be?

If you answered yes to any of these questions you are giving away your power and being a victim. (And right about now you want to punch me. But hear me out first!)

Here's an easy formula

(Note that this is *not a philosophical statement* but a simple mathematical equation that anyone can test)

We are free to the same extent that we are willing to take personal responsibility for our life and experience.

In other words:

The level of freedom we experience is directly proportional to the level of responsibility we are willing to take for our life and our experience.

Let me explain

In every event, reaction, issue or challenge where we blame others or circumstance, and for which we do *not* take responsibility, by definition we remain a powerless *victim*. (Let's be clear about something: we all do this, and it is absolutely okay!) Where we start to take responsibility we move from victimhood and being a passive object (life – or our reality – happens to us) to an active doer (we make life – or our reality – happen), rediscovering and exercising our freedom to choose. Everything we do, think, feel and perceive is a choice we make, either consciously or unconsciously.

Remember that taking responsibility is *not about blaming or shaming ourselves*. Stopping the blame and taking responsibility for our experience means that we reclaim our power over it. Each time we think our suffering is the fault of our circumstance or other people, we give our power away. By default, we remain a victim to the situation.

It is much easier to take responsibility when things are going our way, and more challenging when they aren't, or when we are in pain.

I never used to consciously think of myself as a victim; in fact, quite the opposite. Owning my hidden sense of victimhood was one of the hardest things for me to do.

Blaming my husband, his health problems and family issues, for example, was an excuse for me to remain victimized and avoid taking responsibility for my own pain. Admitting that – and much more – was confronting to say the least, but it has been one of the main things that changed everything.

Nobody can make us feel anything

I was reminded by my dear teacher that we can always take responsibility for our inner experience and emotions. Even though I had known this on an intellectual level, when the going got tough I had slipped back into blaming. Frankly, I still have a tendency to do this!

I'm always freed by the realization that I am in charge of my life: I have the power and the freedom to choose how I interpret things and what I do about them. I am the creator of my own story. Even if I don't like the choices I have in a given moment, I always have some.

To come out of victimhood is to remember your power!

Besides our actions, feelings, thoughts and inner reality we can also take responsibility for our external, physical reality such as our health, wealth, relationships – anything really.

It is my responsibility to change those things that don't work for me that I *can* change, and either accept or leave the situations that I can't change. I can do the former by speaking my truth, setting healthy boundaries that work for me, and making conscious, proactive choices in relationships, work, family, self-care and so on.

It can be tempting to use personal responsibility as an excuse not to speak our truth to each other when it's confronting, or set appropriate boundaries or hold each other accountable. But true personal responsibility requires actions such as these.

More radically, we can even extend the practice of taking responsibility to the things that seem to *happen to us*, the things we attract into our life and energy field. The more we do this, the more we notice that the inner and outer worlds are completely connected. Mastering this can take quite a bit of practice! Go slowly and make sure not to turn it into a self shaming or blaming exercise along the lines of, 'I must have done something wrong to have brought this illness onto myself' (or worse yet, do it to someone else). A healthier, more functional version could be, 'How may I have contributed to my illness, and what lifestyle changes can I make to aid my recovery?' Or if we always end up in the same kind of dysfunctional relationships or with similar (unavailable / abusive / disloyal / fill the blank) partners, it is time to investigate why we keep attracting – or being attracted to – them. Responsibility isn't a reason to blame ourselves (it's all because of me / it's all my shit) or blame them (it's all because of you / it's all your shit), but a reason to find out how we are contributing to our unwanted patterns and take necessary actions to change them.

My business and your business

It is good to remember that we are *not responsible* for other people's inner experience. It is theirs to own – or *not* own, as the case may be! It is not our business to impose the practice of taking personal responsibility on anyone. In fact a lot of people choose not to take responsibility for much more than is legally or socially required of them, and that's okay too.

It is just helpful to remember that you have a choice. If you are dedicated to setting yourself truly free, you'll soon find out that taking *responsibility* is something you can't bypass. It's a powerful internal practice towards your own personal freedom.

How to practice taking profound personal responsibility

Obviously taking 100% responsibility for *everything* you experience is a big call; so be understanding with yourself. 'Grow the muscle' bit by bit, and try to have a sense of humor about it. Otherwise it'll be too easy to slip into shaming or blaming yourself when you fail, or when things don't go your way. Start with the easier things and explore more deeply at your own pace, as you genuinely feel willing and ready. Some things will be much harder to take responsibility for than others.

When brought into consciousness, our unconscious patterns and behaviors that cause our suffering start to lose their power over us and eventually cease to exist.

Freedom is the will to be responsible for ourselves.[6]
Friedrich Nietzsche

Get to know and love your shadow

As the name suggests, the 'shadow self' is the part of us that is in the dark: the part that we have denied, suppressed or hidden away, even from ourselves. It's the part we have decided not to be like because somewhere, somehow, we decided that it is not okay; that it is bad, wrong, stupid or unsafe.

Over many years of personal development work I hadn't realized that I was creating tighter and tighter requirements for myself on how I should be, live and behave. I didn't know that in the quest of becoming a 'better person' I was rejecting a larger and larger part of myself; hence almost growing and developing my defense rather than my knowing, acceptance and love of myself.

And what's the problem with this? Because all those parts of our psyche and emotions that are in the dark actually have great power over us. They can keep us stuck.

As babies we do not have a shadow. Young children simply express who they are without hiding their feelings or censoring their thoughts or actions. As we grow up we start to regulate our emotions and actions, but also put more and more of ourselves in the shadow, the unconscious part, and lock it away.

The thing is, the bigger the shadow, the less we are able to be and love ourselves. Hence in our endeavor to be happy and free; to change undesirable patterns and transform our life; getting familiar with our shadow is of utmost importance and benefit.

Bringing light into darkness

If the shadow is hidden and unconscious, then how can you become aware of it? How can you bring light into that which is in the dark?

A good way to get to know those hidden parts of yourself is through your judgments of others. Yup! Each time you are triggered by someone or their actions, instead of making them wrong, you can take the opportunity to have a look at yourself. What you don't like in others is usually the same things you don't like about, or have disowned, in yourself.

Often painful emotions get pushed into the shadow. We avoid feeling and working through them by denying that they are there in the first place. But when we are being reactive these shadow emotions get exposed.

Another sign of a hidden part could be those qualities that we admire or envy in others, but think we could never be like. Sometimes really beautiful, golden parts get pushed into the shadow. Maybe our creativity was shut off as a child because someone told us that it was a waste of time or that we weren't doing it right. Perhaps we suppressed our playfulness because we were under pressure to grow up too fast, or our parents told us we were being too loud, too messy or childish. Maybe we shut off parts of our sexuality because it was labeled dirty or a sin. Maybe we blocked off our love because we'd been hurt too many times and decided it wasn't safe.

The perfectionism trap

If you have a tendency for perfectionism and being hard on yourself when making the smallest mistake, or when falling short of a high expectation, you probably have a particularly large part in the shadow. Because of the hidden nature of those qualities, they will not be obvious. You may even think you have no shadow at all. In this case it will take even deeper digging to get in touch with it.

Another foolproof way to reveal your blind spots is through honest feedback from others – as hard as it is to receive. Even if you strongly disagree, when multiple people see you a certain way it is worth listening and investigating what it is that you aren't seeing yourself. You'll probably be tempted to brush it off with 'that's definitely not true', but if you feel uncomfortable with the feedback then there's a high chance that they see something about you that you are in being blind to. Uncomfortability is always a top clue!

Sometimes a part of your shadow self gets revealed accidentally. When you react or behave in a way that is out of character, or that feels like, 'That just wasn't me – I don't know where that came from!', it was actually a part of your shadow that revealed itself and caught you off guard.

Find the hidden treasures

What can keep us from accepting our shadow parts is the fear that in accepting them we would be letting them grow and take over our lives. However almost the opposite is true: when we become aware of something it can no longer run us unconsciously, and, as soon as we accept it, we are free to choose; it loses its power over us.

Resistance keeps us energetically locked whereas acceptance releases the bind.

When we begin to dig out, dust off and polish all of those parts that we have judged and made wrong, we'll find that they also have positive aspects and useful, healthy expressions.

In disowning our anger we may have forgotten our ability to say no, set healthy boundaries or protect ourselves. In locking away parts of our sexuality we may have blocked or limited our ability to connect deeply and intimately. In denying our laziness we may have forgotten how to relax.

Finding the healthy, golden qualities amongst them helps us love and accept all the hidden parts!

Reclaim your wholeness

When beginning to explore and reclaim those parts of yourself that you have hidden away, it's important to do so in a safe, private space, in a non-shaming environment away from everyday consequences. This could be alone with a diary or in a group of people where you feel safe to express things that are confronting or uncomfortable.

As a result of working with your shadow, you'll feel more comfortable in your own skin, more confident and happy in who you are, and safer to share yourself with others. With less of you hidden away, you reclaim your sense of wholeness.

People who are open to exploring and exposing their shadow are able to have more connection and intimacy in their relationships as they are able to see and let themselves be seen more fully, without the restrictive masks behind which the shadow hides.

PRACTICE FOR GETTING TO KNOW YOUR SHADOW

Take pen and paper. Think about something that triggered you lately – anything big or small that caused a reaction in you, either internal or external. Write down your ugliest, most secret thoughts and feelings about it. Don't water it down; don't sweeten it up!

Remember this is only an exercise for getting to know your shadow self. Keep going as long as you have something to write. Then read it to yourself without judgment (if you can) and notice the feelings that come up about the text. Write them down too. Then feel free to rip, burn or throw away the piece of paper, or keep it safe if you prefer.

Remember the aim of the exercise is to reveal more of yourself to yourself, to get to know yourself better.

*Knowing your own darkness is the best method for
dealing with the darkness of other people.*[7]
Carl Jung

Heart-centered living – connecting to the wisdom of the heart

You must have heard the sayings 'I know it in my heart' or 'Listen to your heart.' When we live only in the head, we are effectively cut off from the part of ourselves that allows us to access our intuitive and infinitely wise inner knowing.

Heart-centered living means living with that intelligent awareness and intuitive knowing that can be accessed only through a connection to the heart.

Besides being a muscle that pumps blood throughout the body, the heart is a major information processing center with its own nervous system and its own hormone-generating center. Better heart-brain synchronization improves all our cognitive ability, influencing our perception and decision-making.

Are you living in the heart?

- Do you experience periods of hope, appreciation, acceptance and/or peace on a daily basis?
- Do you automatically look for the mutually best solution to all parties in any circumstance?

- Do you spontaneously look for ways to show love to others and to yourself?
- Do you often feel happy for no particular reason?
- Do you find yourself in a state of acceptance of others' behavior a lot of the time?
- Do you want for your (partner, spouse, child, etc.) that which they want for themselves?
- Do you truly treat others as you desire to be treated?
- Do you find it easy to identify with or feel compassion for other people's points of view and circumstances?

Heart vs. Head

Did you know that there is much more information going from the body to the brain than from the brain to the body?

The logical mind is a very valuable tool in most areas of our life. But relying only on the head and abandoning the emotional heart as if it were something weak or secondary can leave us feeling alone and isolated (even in a big city surrounded by millions of people, or with a thousand friends on Facebook!).

It is through the heart that we connect to everything. When it comes to love and intimacy, the heart is our access point. Cutting ourselves off from our heart means cutting ourselves from love. Heart-based living nurtures us mentally, emotionally, physically and spiritually.

One of the reasons we often avoid the heart and stay predominantly in the head is because we escape into constant thinking to avoid feeling. It is through the body that we feel and through the emotional heart specifically that we connect to our vulnerability.

Even if we feel pain or discomfort when we enter the heart it is nothing compared to the pain and wounding we will have to suffer if we keep avoiding it.

Listening to our heart means honoring ourselves. It can involve some deep level, open and honest inner work. In the heart there are no rules – the only rules are those that we make up ourselves. However our heart will never guide us the wrong way.

When relating with other people, instead of getting caught up in the story of who said or did what and our judgments of it, if we notice how it makes us *feel* – and communicate that – we create an opening for a more vulnerable, heart-based connection. We say 'heart to heart' for a reason!

We are multi-dimensional beings, which means that to live to our highest potential, we cannot abandon or deny any part of our being; our heart, our mind or our soul.

SIMPLE PRACTICE TO CONNECT TO YOUR HEART

Take time to sit or lie down quietly, simply relaxing with eyes closed. Allow your breath to be free, and notice it naturally slowing down and deepening as you relax more and more. Let your attention drop from your head, your thoughts and all the internal commentary, down to your body.

First just be aware of the whole body and how it feels. Then start bringing your attention specifically to the area of your heart. Simply sit (or lie) and breathe, focusing gently on the heart center. Direct your breath to that area as if you were breathing straight in and out of your heart.

If your mind gets distracted and occupied by thoughts, keep guiding your attention back to your breath and your heart each time.

Love is the opposite of fear and love lives in the heart.
Unknown

Invitation to a new paradigm: a reality of your choice

How is it possible that two people can see, experience and interpret exactly the same situation in such different ways, and feel contrary feelings about it? How can our individual experience of reality vary so much; even be contradictory? Does that make one right and the other wrong?

Relativity in daily life

Have you experienced or witnessed a situation where two people account the same set of events in completely different ways? They have diverse versions of how things happened, and both are convinced their version is true. They cannot fathom how the other person doesn't see things the way they do.

She says this and he says that – heads butt

The different ways in which we interpret reality can be an endless source of conflict in relationships. Hence we often like to hang out with people who experience reality similarly to us, and we often misunderstand, judge or feel threatened by people who do not.

However, as an alternative to this conflict, we might come to the conclusion that our realities are always our individual interpretation – not correct or incorrect – just different. Centuries-old yogic and Buddhist texts speak about the relativity of our reality. Philosophers have always been interested in it and quantum mechanics is investigating it today, finding scientific proof.

We can also explore the nature of our reality right here in our own lives.

Shaping our reality

It may look like it is our circumstance that keeps us stuck where we are: if it weren't for our health, our kids, our parents, our responsibilities or the current political situation, our life would be freer. However, most of the time it's not the circumstances themselves that keep us stuck, but the beliefs we have around them, and the choices we make based on them: all the *shoulds* and the *have-tos* that we see as real.

I've witnessed in my own life and those of others that true transformation and freedom starts from within – and what we believe about ourselves and the world not only influences how we interpret life, but actually plays a part in shaping our physical, external reality, including our health, wealth, relationships and success.

I invite you to at least imagine for a moment that this is the case:

Would you be ready to move from a life of stress, anxiety, depression or difficult relationships to a new reality of deep fulfillment, ease and emotional freedom? How does that idea make you feel? What are the resisting thoughts that come up?

You can have financial freedom, be free to travel wherever you want, do whatever you wish with your life and choose with whom to share it – have all the right circumstances – but still be a prisoner to your own mind, fears, defenses and emotional pain.

Just to clarify, I'm not just talking about learning to control your mind or control your emotions, or manage your stress or your anger, but I am talking about true freedom; a whole new reality! How does that sound to you?

The way to get there may be so surprising and so against your current paradigm that you actually resist it to begin with.

It's crazy, but we hang onto our shitty story and old limited reality of misery, hardship, illness and lack of love, gathering proof and evidence to back it up like our life depends on it – I know I did! Otherwise we would all be walking around in bliss and love all the time!

From paradigm paralysis to miracles

When we live in a certain kind of personal reality – be it one of busyness, struggle, emotional or physical pain, disease, injustice or heart-wrenching relationship drama – it can be hard to see past it to the possibility of a different kind of reality. Especially when masses of people live and believe in the same reality – like the almightiness of modern medical science – it is easy to get stuck in that dominant paradigm.

The inability or refusal to see beyond our current models of thinking is called 'paradigm paralysis'.

When we finally step outside of that reality and expand our views beyond what is generally believed possible, so-called miracles happen! That which is thought impossible suddenly becomes possible. When more people begin to cross that border, the whole collective paradigm shifts.

Think of the four-minute mile which was considered impossible until Roger Bannister achieved it in 1954. Soon after him it was broken by more athletes and now it is considered a standard for male professional middle distance runners. It is a good example of a collective shift that happens after the shift of one individual.

Make shift happen

Shifting your paradigm isn't to be confused with denial. A paradigm shift is very deep and happens on all levels of your being; conscious, unconscious, mental, emotional and even physical.

Denial on the other hand is just our conscious mind denying and covering up what is happening in our unconscious mind, and emotional or physical body.

Remember that in order to step into this new reality you have to own and let go of the old beliefs about yourself and the world that kept you stuck in the first place. It can be scary because somehow you believe that they keep you safe; after all it is what you have been certain of all your life, perhaps for generations.

Often we are so unconscious of our story and so used to living it that we really believe it is the only possible truth.

But paradigm shift can happen in an unexpected way: We may not be miraculously cured from a serious illness, but our relationship with it could change dramatically. Something that used to seem like a life sentence could turn into a blessing.

Freedom – nothing less

It can be really confronting to uncover those deeply hidden emotions and aspects of yourself that you never accepted or wanted to admit to anyone, but they need to be revealed and owned before you can choose to move beyond them. It is challenging and terrifying at first to start taking responsibility for your experience.

I call you to open your mind and your heart – and I promise you it will all be worth it. It means freedom – nothing less.

P.S. I just want to remind you that there is nothing wrong with you (or your pain); there never was and never will be. We are all born with limitless potential. When you learn to love yourself fully your whole world transforms and reflects it back to you a thousandfold. Your true connection and intimacy with yourself opens up your connection to everything outside of you; other people, nature and spirit.

Believe it or not, it is your choice!

WHAT BELIEFS LIMIT YOUR CURRENT REALITY?

Take pen and paper and write down some of your wildest dreams – or wildest dreams you ever had, even if you have given up on them by now.

Then write:

- But that isn't realistic because…
- But I can't have this because…
- And this is not possible because….
- Which is because….

And keep going like this until you can't get any further! The deeper you go the more limiting beliefs you will uncover. You might even argue that some of them are facts, and they may be, *for now!* Remember that anything can be a fact – until it's not. And this is the point: the current facts are just the current collective belief.

You might say that that also is just a belief, not a fact, which is quite right. But what kind of beliefs would you rather have, those that limit your world and keep you stuck and unhappy, or those that set you free?

Truth is not a belief. You can believe whatever you want – it need not have anything to do with reality. If you make a large number of people believe something, lies will become mainstream. Once you believe, your entire identity will be built on what you believe. Belief leads people to accept the most ridiculous things as the absolute truth.[8]
Sadghuru

Breath and the self-healing body

Why have I included a chapter on breathing in a book about emotional freedom? Because breathing is possibly our most undervalued resource of the body: It is an in-built release and healing mechanism that has the power to transform our life, health and relationships from the inside out.

The breath factor

Could something as simple and automatic as our breath really be the key to easing anxiety, emotional issues, and even depression? Could it be that we already have the solution to the numerous stress-related health problems built into our physical body?

If so, then why are increasing numbers of people struggling with chronic stress, anxiety, and a multitude of related issues? I will attempt to answer these questions, and more, in this chapter!

Stress breath syndrome

Have you ever observed what happens to your breath when you are stressed? Yes; it gets short and shallow, maybe out of rhythm. The chest is tight: you automatically tense your muscles and restrict your breathing.

Habitually tensing muscles and breathing insufficiently result in less blood flow and subsequently less oxygen in the body.

When this goes on for long periods of time, the body needs to use the available oxygen primarily for vital body functions, and non-vital functions get second place. The ongoing lack of oxygen disturbs our digestion, circulation, metabolism, reproduction and all normal body functions, which leads to physical illness, chronic pain, headaches, and so on.

There is also a relationship between blood oxygen levels and production of serotonin (the mood regulating neurotransmitter). Restricted breathing and low serotonin levels lead to even more tension and less optimal breathing. The effect snowballs and the vicious cycle is ready.

Conscious, deep breathing (such as in breathwork therapy or full diaphragmatic breathing) floods the body and cells with oxygen and reverses this cycle.

The difference between breathing and *breathing*

The interesting thing about breathing is that we can do it consciously or unconsciously. We don't have to think about it. We don't have to remember to breathe – we do it automatically anyway. But the practice of conscious breathing has some immense health benefits. This is because the breath is a direct link between the mind and the body, and the parasympathetic (which controls the homeostasis and the 'rest and digest' response), and the sympathetic (which activates the 'fight or flight' mode) nervous systems.

What does that mean in practical terms? As we already established, when we get stressed out our breathing gets faster. But by consciously slowing down and deepening our breath we can also calm down the whole nervous system, our emotions and the state of our mind. Pretty cool, right?

Stress – our archenemy?

Stress is a normal and natural part of life. All humans and animals experience mental, physical, or emotional stress from time to time. Natural levels of short-term stress actually enhance our mental and physical performance.

Prolonged, chronic stress, however, is not our friend. The question is: how do we process and release it, or do we hold on to it and store it in the body?

Animals and young children naturally release stress and emotional charge through automatic mechanisms of the body, such as different spontaneous breathing patterns, sounds, shaking, crying, and so on.

As we grow up, however, we learn to suppress these release mechanisms. Instead of allowing ourselves to fully feel and express all of our emotions, we tense up the body and restrict our breathing as an unconscious defense not to feel our difficult feelings, or show them to others. Outside we may even seem cool, calm and collected, but inside we hold on to the fear, emotional pain, or anger.

Over time the state of stress becomes more and more chronic and habitual; the neurological feedback loops of stress are reinforced again and again. The stress we have not dealt with, plus 'negative' emotions, accumulate and can develop into anxiety, depression, or chronic pain and illness over time.

Trust the body

We live in an era where we are taught to look for most answers from outside of ourselves; we read books, listen to podcasts by various experts, see practitioners, and do courses that give us (often contradictory) advice about how to eat, how to exercise, live, think, parent, relax, achieve our goals, be a better person… you get the picture.

Don't get me wrong. I, too, am a big fan of the information age where all of the above is readily available and it is easy to study or research almost anything remotely from the comfort of your home, favourite café, or anywhere in the world.

But there is something that we are overlooking or forgetting about in the process: the infinite wisdom and power that is in us all, already built into the intelligent self-healing mechanism that is our body and mind.

This lack of faith in our body's ability to heal itself is at least partly fuelled by the huge worldwide industry that benefits from our not trusting our bodies or feeling well. Yes, the very the same one that sells a quick-fix drug for each ailment we have.

Reading the messages

All the different physical symptoms we experience in our body are trying to tell us something important. If, instead of listening to those messages, we go straight to our medicine cabinet looking for the solution, we are just putting a plaster on top of a deep, seeping wound.

TV commercials and ads everywhere pound into our heads that we are to take an antacid tablet for our heartburn, a painkiller for our headache, medicated gel for muscle tension and medicinal lozenges for our sore throats or head colds. They ease the symptoms for a while and we go back to feeling normal – until the symptoms return either in the same or a different variation. This is because, even though the symptoms have been momentarily relieved, the underlying issues remain. The wound keeps on weeping and gradually getting worse; it needs to be cleaned from the inside out.

Medicalized emotions

The same over-medicalization also applies to our emotional life. When we feel unhappy for a long time, have lost our mojo, are stressed, sad, or riddled with fear for any reason we can be prescribed an anti-anxiety or anti-depressant medication. Alternatively we may self-medicate with our drug of choice – including alcohol and recreational drugs, even excessive meditation – to feel better or, more accurately, to feel less.

Unfortunately their use doesn't often work in our favour. Many of these drugs, in fact, work to further suppress the body's own natural healing and release mechanisms and inhibit their functions.

Nothing is healed or resolved; only the symptoms have been momentarily numbed out. This is why the medication often doesn't work in the long term. The underlying issues still remain.

Cause of emotional pain and trauma

No one goes through life without experiencing pain or trauma, be it gross and obvious or subtle and more difficult to notice. It is part of human life.

Gross trauma is caused by things like accidents, natural disasters, war, physical or sexual abuse: something 'big' and obviously traumatic.

Gross trauma can sometimes be easier to deal with because it is more obvious, providing that we remember, or at least are aware of, the event. Even then, our conscious mind may often minimise the effect the event has had on us emotionally, yet we carry the imprints in the physical body for years to come. A good example of this is post-traumatic stress disorder (PTSD).

Subtle trauma is often emotional in nature and can be more difficult to pinpoint. It may be as simple as unmet love needs or hearing Mum and Dad fight when we were little. Incidents that may seem insignificant to an adult can often leave strong imprints in the emotional body, which we then carry around as unconscious memories and negative core beliefs for years to come.

The breathing solution

The yogis have used breath as a way to direct, re-balance and transform vital energy (prana or chi / qi) for thousands of years. A lot can be learnt from full yogic (diaphragmatic) breathing. The yogic approach, pranayama, is more about breath control and using breath as a way to control and balance our vital energy: replenish it where it is deficient and move it where it is stagnant.

Breathwork therapy harnesses the body's own natural mechanisms for releasing stress and emotional charge. Simply described, it is emotional release work. It helps the body to naturally let go of our emotional build-up so that we can live free from the negative influences of past traumatic experiences and suppressed emotions and their long-term consequences.

Feeling and physically releasing these emotions results in deep healing and permanent change faster than analysing mental level memories in traditional talk therapy. The technique works through a style of conscious, connected breathing, which you do under the guidance of a trained facilitator.

How does it work?

Breathwork reaches the limbic system to release deep, and often hidden, unconscious emotional trauma or wounding that accumulated in the cell memory of the body over the course of our lives. Hence numerous physical health benefits occur.

The specific style of active, circular breathing (that children do naturally when releasing emotional charge) stimulates the hippocampus, the part of the brain that stores our painful memories, and the amygdala, which is responsible for our emotions and other functions related to anxiety and depression. As a result, our built-up emotional pain is brought to the surface to be felt, processed and released.

During a breathwork session we may have profound and intense emotional experiences, or have emotional memories of past events that we have blocked out of our consciousness. This is why it's important to do it under the guidance of an experienced and qualified breathwork practitioner who can support us safely and skilfully through the process.

Breathwork therapy also includes conscious counseling and mental processing techniques. These help us to uncover and let go of the subconscious negative core beliefs that keep our unwanted patterns running and hold us back in life.

What are the benefits?

Breathwork helps the body to naturally let go of emotional build-up so that we can live free from the negative influences of past traumatic experiences and suppressed emotions and their long-term consequences. It goes far beyond the approach of 'emotional management' and instead helps us use our powerful emotions as a resource; not just something to be controlled.

As the emotional and somatic (physical) body clear, the whole nervous system is cleansed and re-set and all our energies begin to flow freely again. You will find you have more energy available to take care of tasks in daily life and do more of the things you love. Breathwork therapy offers real relief from anxiety, depression, and all emotional issues.

This leads to easier and more fulfilling relationships and deeper intimacy. When we are no longer re-creating and acting from our past trauma and the defenses built around it, our relationships – both with ourselves and with others – become much richer and more real. We are finally able to release our unconscious negative beliefs, break through repetitive negative patterns and exchange them for more functional and fulfilling ones.

The quality of our breath expresses our inner feelings.[9]
TKV Desikachar

PART 2

Relationships

Break through defenses and connect authentically

What keeps us from being real in relationships and how it can screw things up.

We've all been there: in our heart we love someone – either despite or because of who they are or what they have done – but something in us holds back from expressing it fully. We withhold our love, protect ourselves, build up walls, close off or pretend.

We don't consciously want to, but somehow it just happens. Perhaps we have been hurt in the past and don't want it to happen again. Perhaps we are cautious not to be too happy in case it all falls apart. Perhaps we think we have to be someone or something else to get their attention and love.

When we are not being fully ourselves – in other words, when we are acting from our defense – we are unable to connect deeply and authentically. As a result we can feel very alone even when not alone.

So what is it that keeps us from being real around other people, even those we love? What is it that makes us try to be what we think we should be, or what we think people need or want us to be, rather than be authentically and genuinely ourselves in every moment?

Fear is the opposite of love

You may have heard a saying that fear is the opposite of love, but what does it actually mean in real life? Fear often makes us act and relate to others from our *defense* – our defense against the fear (of being hurt, criticized, rejected or made wrong). In fear we behave *so that…*

In fear we gather evidence and read things into other people's actions; we try to figure out what they mean and what their intentions are, and how we should respond to get the reaction we want, and in order to keep ourselves safe and keep everyone happy. In fear we try to protect ourselves. We calculate and compare past experiences trying to predict the future and control outcomes.

In love (without fear) we simply trust. We trust ourselves and we trust each other enough to allow ourselves to authentically express our thoughts, feelings, needs and desires without too many filters and *shoulds*.

We know we cannot control another person's thoughts or feelings – so we allow them to express themselves freely, without needing them to be a certain way. If one path fails we take another direction. We don't base our expectations of the future on things that have happened in the past. In love we know that each situation is new and that what happened in the past doesn't have to affect us any more. It may still do, but it doesn't have to.

But what is this fear about? What should we do with it?

Should we just ignore it, deny it, keep a stiff upper lip, keep calm and carry on?

We all have our particular flavors of fear, but there are a few classic ones most of us can relate to – fear of being:

- hurt
- abandoned

- rejected
- not loved
- criticized
- ridiculed
- shamed.

We have fear of loss and fear of death. Most fears, on a deeper level, go under one of these categories. Whatever the fear is, the thing that actually keeps us stuck is not the fear itself, but, paradoxically, the *denial* of it: we build a defense around it. We deny that it is fear – an emotion – and turn it into something concrete.

We gather evidence to back it up and build a convincing case so that we can justify feeling it and make the story a fact (instead of admitting, 'I am afraid of X…', we say, 'X is dangerous because…!'). This is how we actually manifest our fears into physical reality.

Sometimes we defend ourselves by acting and behaving in totally the opposite way to how we feel deep inside. Have you ever found yourself acting over-confidently or even arrogantly in a situation where you actually (if you're really honest with yourself) feel insecure or unsafe? Have you ever noticed yourself pulling away – or pushing others away – when what you really deeply wanted was to be loved, held and noticed?

Subconsciously we think our defenses keep us safe. We think they protect us from the hurt, the pain and whatever it is we fear. But in acting from our defense we are manifesting the very thing we fear!

Express – don't suppress!

We all have our defenses, some more obvious than others. The way to break through them is to acknowledge them, and to investigate what it is that they are covering up.

When we catch ourselves behaving in a way that doesn't feel completely authentic and in line with who we are – when we act from the *so that* intention rather than from a genuine expression of what we think and feel, we can have a look at what lies underneath. If we are acting as if we didn't care when we actually feel hurt, we may find that we are covering up the hurt so that we wouldn't be judged, or so that the other person doesn't know they have this effect on us, or so that our pride and ego don't get hurt as well.

We all have our own individual patterns, but with some time and inner inquiry we can begin to identify what they are.

Often this awareness alone helps to start breaking the patterns, but the real game-changer is expressing our findings to the person involved: instead of reacting from our defended fearful self, actually expressing how we feel and what we are defending against, no matter how silly it seems. This may of course not always be appropriate in a work setting, but it is a breakthrough in all our intimate and personal relationships. It's a challenge, but well worth it!

When we communicate and own our deeper feelings to each other, we are making ourselves vulnerable. It is through this vulnerability and letting ourselves be seen that we are able to truly connect with one another, heart to heart.

From this open and expanded space deep, intimate connection flows. The love dissolves the fear.

PRACTICE

Next time you notice yourself getting triggered by your partner, close friend or family member, take a few deep breaths and drop into your body (you may need to remove yourself from the situation for a moment to do this!). Ask yourself, 'What am I actually feeling?' Drop the story (who said or did what and what you make it mean in your head) and get to the bottom of it. Resist the temptation to react in your usual way. Even if it is to 'not react' but to coil up, go silent and withdraw, that is still a reaction.

Remember the reaction is usually caused by the defense; not the feeling itself. Drop into the feeling. When you feel ready – usually once the trigger has lost some of its charge – go back to the person and communicate how you are feeling, from a place of openness rather than accusation, and watch what happens. This is of course easier said than done; so just know that it gets easier with practice – lots of it!

Authenticity is the daily practice of letting go of who we think we are supposed to be, and embracing who we are.[10]
Brené Brown

Three steps to getting your needs met

Everyone wants to have their needs met.
Here's how to make it happen.

Human beings can survive in very different, even adverse, conditions by cunningly adapting to our environment. We can survive starved of good nutrition or starved of love. However, in order to thrive rather than just survive, we need more optimal nourishment. Like everything in nature, the better nourished we are, the better we thrive, inside and out!

When we were little we were completely dependent on our parents or primary caregivers. This was the time when we learnt, amongst many other things, about having our needs met.

If all or most of our early needs for food, shelter, protection, love and affection, etc., were promptly met, we were more likely to learn that we have the ability to get what we need in life.

Unmet needs

If certain needs were rarely or hardly ever met, we were likely to learn that, no matter what, we cannot get what we need and it is not worth trying.

Here's an example: In young babies that are left to 'cry it out', the activation of the freeze response eventually makes them stop crying (it could be potentially dangerous to keep crying and attracting attention of predators).

When this is repeated regularly the baby learns by conditioning that no matter how much they cry, nobody will come and their needs will not be met – so they give up trying. This is called *learnt helplessness* (a condition that predisposes us to a variety of mental health issues later on in life).[11]

If, as children, we had to work hard to get our needs met, we developed different methods to get what we wanted and needed – and some coping mechanisms for when we didn't. Perhaps we learnt that we got Mum's love and attention by being sick, or being helpless, or by tantruming, or bossing her around – or by being a 'good' girl or boy.

Thus we understood that there are *conditions* to being loved (because, consciously or unconsciously, we equate having our needs met to being loved).

We also learnt to completely deny and block off unmet needs as a defense mechanism. This is how our defenses are born.

And how to meet them

Step 1. Identify your needs

If your needs as a child were frequently not met and you learnt to shut off the unmet needs altogether in order to get by and to numb out the associated pain, it may take a lot of digging to actually identify your needs and get clear about what they are in the first place.

Good indications for unmet needs are repeated situations where you feel less than fulfilled. Are you settling for less, or going for everything you want in life?

Do you stay in an unfulfilling relationship, job or situation because you're afraid it's the best you can get?

Do you think it's wrong or useless to want for something more, or to ask for what you want and need?

Here's a personal example

Both my parents worked long hours from very early on in my life. Even though they were very loving when they were around, over the years I missed out on some parental nurturing and emotional support.

In order to cope I learnt to take care of myself from a young age. I always got myself up, dressed and fed before school, even walked myself to kindergarten at the age of five. In a lot of ways this served me in life, but it also held me back.

Alone I was a functional adult but in relationships I felt depleted and alone. I was often the one supporting the other, but since I didn't trust anyone to be there for me, I never allowed myself to be to supported, emotionally or otherwise – until I got clear about the needs that I had shut off, and began to meet them myself and communicate them to my partner and other important people in my life.

Helpful questions to identify your needs could be

- What are the things missing in my intimate relationship(s)?
- What am I always left wanting more of?
- What do I feel like I am missing out on in my relationship or job or life?

Step 2. Meet your own needs

It is important to remember that, now that we are grownups, we have the ability to meet our own needs; that we are not dependent on others to fill them all like when we were little – nor is it reasonable to expect it. So if we didn't get enough love and nurturing in our childhood (or enough encouragement, acceptance, protection…) it is up to *us* to start giving them to ourselves first!

It helps to be really honest about where you are not giving yourself what you need; sacrificing or belittling your needs, even making them wrong.

Once you have identified the need, you might want to ask yourself what would having it met actually look like in action. Be aware that your adult mind might try to rationalize the need away; so speak directly from your heart, the vulnerable part of you.

The answers may surprise you! If it is protection or safety you needed, it could look like standing up for yourself more at work or in relationships, or taking better care of your finances. If you need more love and intimacy it could look like making more time for friends and loved ones in your life, or doing more things that you love alone: a personal yoga practice, or taking time to meditate or play the guitar, or spending time being intimate with yourself. If you need nurturing and caring it could look like making sure you eat well, rest well and generally improve your level of self-care. Remember that the answers will be individual.

In close relationships we tend to look for what we haven't learnt to give ourselves

If I always end up feeling like I am not loved for who I am, then chances are I am not loving myself as who I am. If I feel unsupported by my partner or friends, the likelihood is that there is a part of me that isn't supporting myself; hence I look for it in them.

Or if I am overly critical of myself, I will also be overly sensitive to criticism from others, and will easily interpret as criticism something that was not meant as such.

Once we learn to meet our own needs and love ourselves the way we need to be loved, we stop having to constantly look for it outside of ourselves.

Step 3. Express your needs

- Are you sometimes aware that you want or need something, but don't voice it?

- Do you often feel like you don't have the 'right' to ask for what you want?

- Do you put the needs of others before your own and end up feeling depleted and eventually resentful?

- Do you sometimes not voice your needs because you don't want to 'bother' the other person or don't expect them to be interested? Or do you think they should know what you need without you telling them?

- Do you think you deserve more and keep waiting for others to notice?

A good rule of thumb in all relationships is that we have the *right to ask but no right to demand*. Asking includes no obligation, and it actually requires vulnerability. This is why it can be hard, but also incredibly rewarding.

Even the Bible says, 'Ask, and it will be given to you.'[12] This specifically indicates that we do need to ask and voice our needs. When we voice our needs and desires we add energy into them. When we have trouble expressing our needs we are more likely to resort to manipulation.

It may be tempting to assume, 'If she/he really loved me they would know what I need or want'. However, since we are all different, we also have different needs (apart from the basic ones we all share). In order to feel loved, supported, accepted, etc., we also need it to be shown to us in differing ways.

When we voice our needs clearly, without expectation, we are actually letting the other person in, allowing them to be there for us and meet our need, if it feels right for them. This can be an opportunity for a new level of connection; a beautiful gift both ways!

You will be your best self when you take time to understand what you really need, feel and want.[13]
Deborah Day

Creating healthy boundaries

Boundaries are what keep us safe in all our relationships; be it at work, within our family or our circle of friends. Lack of healthy boundaries will cause us to lose ourselves and become disempowered and feel like we don't have a choice.

Let's start with a few questions

- Do you often find yourself saying yes to something, but secretly wanting to say no, or saying yes reluctantly (with a 'but…') and with a feeling of uneasiness?
- Are you very sensitive to other people's moods and / or highly affected by them?
- Do you often feel responsible for making or keeping others happy, or worry about upsetting people?
- Do you find yourself either snowed under with work or burdened by things you are doing for other people at the expense of your own well-being, personal time and energy?
- Do you sometimes say that it's fine, when actually it's not, and then make the other person or their actions wrong in your head, or feel hurt but don't communicate it?

If you answered yes to one or more of the questions, chances are you can benefit from working on your personal boundaries!

INTERNAL AND EXTERNAL BOUNDARIES

A personal boundary is a sort of imaginary line between you and others. It divides what's yours from what's somebody else's. That applies not only to your body, money, and belongings, but also to your inner reality, feelings, thoughts and needs. It's the border between my business and your business.

Our boundaries can be both internal and external.

Internal boundaries

An internal boundary has to do with protecting our sense of self and knowing the difference between my feelings and my reality vs. your feelings and your reality. It means knowing that I am entitled to my personal experience, different from yours (and vice versa) and that your emotional state doesn't have to affect mine – nor is it my responsibility.

When our internal boundaries are not in place we feel strongly affected by other people's emotions and their opinions of us and everything else. We may react by building thick walls around ourselves and shutting people out or making them wrong when they don't agree with us or when we don't see things the same way.

Or we feel the need to seek for others' approval and to 'keep everyone happy'. We may be overly worried about upsetting other people, at the expense of being true to ourselves. We may feel obligated to keep constantly giving to others until we are exhausted.

All of the above are also symptoms of a lack of healthy self-esteem. When we don't have sufficient self-esteem we easily become addicted to 'other-esteem', meaning our sense of self-worth is dependent on the approval of others, or our success in their eyes. In the process of people-pleasing it is easy to forget about our own boundaries and lose our power.

Sometimes lack of internal boundaries is mistaken as compassion, but the difference is that real compassion or sympathy doesn't leave us feeling miserable, depleted or used. We can have compassion for others without losing ourselves. Compassion allows us to still look after ourselves, stay centered, empowered and to give priority to our happiness and well-being.

External boundaries

An external boundary is about being honest with yourself and others about what's okay for you and what isn't, and getting clear on what kind of treatment you are willing to tolerate.

An important part of external boundaries, therefore, is communicating them to others. One of the most obvious ways to do this is learning to say no when you don't feel fully comfortable saying yes. If you often feel obligated to say yes when you'd really like to say no, this may take a bit of practice!

One of the benefits of practicing this is that when you do say yes you can mean it wholeheartedly. Then it is not a hesitant 'yes' (in reality more like a 'maybe') but a true, committed one. This builds trust within yourself as well as with people around you. Others will actually feel more comfortable asking for anything when they know you feel free to say no when you mean it.

Setting, communicating and respecting personal boundaries, both internal and external, is one of the greatest acts of self-love you can practice.

Healthy boundaries keep us feeling safe in the world and in relationships. They significantly reduce the need for fear, defensiveness and arguments. They help keep our identity intact and avoid enmeshment and codependence where our experience, emotions and actions are overly influenced by those of others.

Exercising healthy boundaries also enables us to be *authentic and transparent* in our relationships, a key to true intimacy.

Stone and sand boundaries

There are also two different kinds of (external) boundaries we have with others – those that are set in stone and those that are not. The 'sand' boundaries are more flexible and open to negotiation; for example, 'I could be willing to work late on occasion, or one evening a week, as long as I know in advance and can make arrangements.'

In reality there are very few stone boundaries. They are those things that we absolutely cannot, or are not willing to, live with. Most of them have to do with safety; for example, physical violence. The more stone boundaries we have, the more we set ourselves and others up for failure and disappointment!

Even with kids the only boundaries that really need to be set in stone are those related to safety. Most other things can be at least a little bit flexible depending on circumstance, or at least can be discussed and agreed on together.

The communication

Communicating boundaries is not about making demands, making anyone wrong or telling other people what to do. It is about expressing clearly, without blaming, what is okay for us and what isn't. Since individual boundaries can be so different and other people may take time to respond to them, they may need to be communicated and negotiated time and time again.

In a partnership we are often required to reflect on what is fundamental to us and what isn't – what we are willing to live with and what we are not. Ultimately respecting our own boundaries could even mean leaving a relationship where our boundaries are crossed again and again.

As we as people grow and change, our boundaries can also change and be re-negotiated as required. Especially with family members who are used to our being a certain way, setting new boundaries can take some patience! When our boundaries are in place we become a lot less reactive.

Finding the boundary

Knowing where the 'correct' boundary lies is not something anyone outside of you can answer – not even your best friend. It is always a question you need to ask yourself, along the lines of:

- Does this feel right for me?
- What am I honestly okay or not okay with?
- Do I *want* to say yes or no?
- How do I *really* feel about this?
- Does this sit with me morally and ethically?

Boundaries are a very personal thing and what is totally okay in one relationship may be unacceptable in another. There is no universal right or wrong here; we are all entitled to our own limits that work for us individually.

The positive flip-side of strengthening our personal boundaries is that we automatically become more respectful of other people's boundaries. We begin to respect the personal reality of others and realize that it is not our job to try to change anyone, their experience or their emotions, or to rescue or control anyone, but to value, appreciate and have faith in the differences in each other.

Healthy boundaries are one of the biggest gifts we can give ourselves, and others, in all our relationships.

PRACTICE

Next time you hear yourself saying it's fine when you don't meant it 100% (and don't kid yourself that you never do that!) or saying yes when there is a 'but' or a condition, stop!

If you need to take some time to get clear on how you feel about it, you can say, 'Can I think about this?' – and then get clear! Listen to your inner voice. Are you saying yes because it feels too hard to say no? Or because you don't want to upset your friend? Because you feel you *should*? Then go back and practice saying no.

When we fail to set boundaries and hold people accountable, we feel used and mistreated. This is why we sometimes attack who they are, which is far more hurtful than addressing a behavior or a choice.[14]
Brené Brown

Mastering the art of conscious communication

Learn to speak your truth clearly — the art of conscious communication.

You've probably heard that communication is key in all relationships. But how is it that what you say and what the other person hears are not always the same thing?

Speaking our truth may sound like an obvious thing. Most of us think that we are pretty truthful and don't tend to lie. However, through a deeper investigation we may find otherwise!

Here are some questions to help:
- How often do you need some help / encouragement / space / loving touch / a salary raise / fill the blank, but don't voice it?
- How often do you feel hurt, angry or jealous but don't express it, hiding it from the other person?
- How often do you say or do something *so that* the other would respond in a certain way, rather than asking for what you need or want outright?
- Do you give compliments that you don't really mean, or pretend to agree or pretend something else just to make the other person like you or feel better, or to avoid conflict?
- Do you sometimes pretend to listen to somebody while having your mind occupied somewhere outside the conversation?

- Do you sometimes spend time with people you don't actually want to spend time with, or even like?
- Do you find yourself pretending or bending the truth in the name of protecting someone else's feelings?
- How often do you say it's fine, when actually it's not, or say yes when you'd actually like to say no?
- Do you sometimes try to cover up a mistake you know you've made instead of owning up to it?

Speaking our truth in a conscious way is always about *our truth*. It is not about our interpretation of the other person's reality, their actions or their feelings, etc., but about *owning our own*.

Speaking our truth is about examining and communicating what has been triggered in us. It could look like telling the other person when we are hurt, angry or scared.

It's best to avoid saying, 'You are doing this or that', as it is easily perceived as an accusation. Even: '*I feel like* you are (or do) this or that' is really our telling how we perceive the other person, rather than actually owning how we feel. A better example would be: 'I feel unsupported and taken for granted cleaning the house by myself week after week. I feel hurt and angry that you have not offered to help.' This way we are taking ownership of our emotions and recognizing that *nobody has the power to make us feel anything.*

Another good way to start an uncomfortable conversation is to say: '*The story I'm making up in my head is that…*' This way we take ownership of our story and interpretation straight away and don't turn it into an accusation.

Many of our daily conflicts are simply due to lack of direct communication and could be easily avoided. Since we shouldn't expect other people to read our minds it is important to learn to speak our truth, set boundaries and express our feelings and reality in a way that is non-threatening and non-blaming – a way that creates more openness, vulnerability, respect and love between us.

Here are some key things to ensure both sides feel heard and respected.

SIMPLE STEPS TO COMMUNICATING CONSCIOUSLY

Take responsibility

Take responsibility for not just your actions but also your own reality – your thoughts, emotions and experience – without blaming them on anybody or remaining a victim. It means remembering that you have a choice to react, or stay in your power and express yourself clearly and make your own conscious decisions about yourself and your life.

This also means that you are only responsible for your own actions. It is not your responsibility to tell others how they should act or behave. But it *is* your responsibility to set boundaries that work for you.

Stick to the facts

Stick to the facts about what happened, without adding coloring, interpretation or exaggeration. 'You are *always* late' probably isn't a fact. The tendency may also be to add *meaning* to the other person's actions, which usually is just an interpretation (=story), rather than a fact. If you can't let go of the story you could just own it outright by saying 'The story I'm making up in my head is…' This way you aren't stating the story as a fact but as what it is, an interpretation.

One important fact is how you are feeling. So it could go something like this: 'When you are late and don't let me know, I feel unimportant, unloved and angry. The story I make up in my mind is that your work is more important to you.'

Set healthy boundaries

This goes along with taking responsibility and speaking our truth. It means letting the other person know clearly if something isn't okay for you; for example:

- I'm not okay with vacuuming and cleaning the house by myself every week
- I am not okay with being spoken to like this / being lied to / your brother staying with us for months
- It's not okay for me to work late / change shifts again with short notice

In our intimate relationships boundaries can be an ongoing negotiation.

The temptation will be to blame or make the other wrong for their actions. When blamed or made wrong, most of us instantly get on the defense. It is very hard to receive a message when it comes in the form of an accusation.

However, when we are willing to make ourselves vulnerable and express how we feel, we are much more likely to get a resolution or at least understand each other.

This brings us to:

Ask for your needs to be met

This could look as simple as 'I really need your help keeping the house tidy. Could you please help by cleaning up after yourself and taking turns cleaning the bathroom and vacuuming?' or 'I would really like to leave work at 6pm most evenings to go spend time with my kids.'

So often we don't ask for what we need because we think the other 'should know' – or we make our case even more complicated by giving their actions meanings such as 'if they really cared they would / wouldn't...' We may also tell ourselves that we don't want to hurt anyone's feelings – but then we end up hurting our own!

This is one form of codependency. Our unexpressed feelings are bound to come out in some other less direct and constructive way before too long.

It's important to acknowledge that our needs are very different, and we simply can't expect people to know what ours are – no matter how obvious it may seem to us – unless we express them clearly. Love and support can look very different to different people.

Again it is important not to blame or accuse the other, and remember that *asking is not the same as demanding*. Most of us don't respond well to demands or being told what to do. They are violations of another person's boundary. So we can enter a negotiation within the boundaries that we honestly feel okay with.

Active listening

Communication is always a two-way street. Everyone wants and deserves to be heard. Active listening means not only holding ourselves back from cutting someone off mid-sentence, but actually listening to what they have to say without presuming we already know what it is.

A good practice in active listening is to summarize what they have just said and repeat it back to them: 'I'm hearing that you feel unsupported and taken for granted and that you need some more help around the house…' This makes the other person feel heard and understood, which is often halfway there, even if we are not able to fully meet their needs.

Don't over share

There is such a thing as Too Much Information! Venting out all your un-edited feelings and judgements on social media probably isn't such a smart idea. And telling a person whom you've only just met intimate details about your messy divorce or financial troubles may be too much too soon.

Do consider your motives and the possible consequences before communicating. Are you just venting to blow off some steam, to get attention and validation, or to make someone else wrong? Is the relationship or the other person going to benefit from what that you are about to share? Is speaking without filter appropriate, or is it likely to backfire?

Even though difficult topics sometimes need to be discussed for the sake of the relationship, some other things are better left unsaid. For example, sharing your judgements and dislikes about qualities the other person cannot change about themselves is unlikely to lead to anything good. Your partner / relationship is probably not going to benefit from you telling him you wish he was taller!

Non-verbal communication

The majority of our communication consists of our body language, tone of voice, gestures, posture, facial expressions and eye contact. Even if we are saying the 'right' words but not meaning them, the other person will pick up on the lack of sincerity. So stay in the truth!

Sometimes we may think we know what people think or feel without their telling us. However most of the time our 'mind reading' is just a reflection of our own unconscious thoughts or fears; not an actual insight into what is going on in their heads or hearts.

Mastering the art of conscious communication gives you much more personal power, meaning you'll be much less reactive and feel more secure and authentic in all your relationships.

Much unhappiness has come into the world because of bewilderment and things left unsaid.[15]
Fyodor Dostoyevsky

Breaking codependence

Codependence is the root cause of most unhappiness and suffering in your relationships. It's not because of the realtionships – it's because you are so affected by them.

According to the messages of most pop music and movies, loving someone equals addiction: emotional rollercoaster, desperately needing the other, constantly thinking of and obsessing over them, behaving compulsively and being hooked – the kind of love that hurts and where we lose ourselves.

This is a very unhealthy picture, and unfortunately love addiction is one of the common types of *codependence*. But codependence doesn't plague us in just romantic relationships. It is where most issues and pain stems from in all types of relationships.

Codependence is a pattern of behavior in which our self-worth and identity are dependent on approval from someone else.

Do you recognize some of these signs?

Low self-esteem

Feeling that you're not good enough, or constant comparing of yourself to others are signs of low self-esteem. The tricky thing about self-esteem is that we can think highly of ourselves – as a disguise of actually feeling unlovable or inadequate underneath.

Perfectionism can hide our feelings of shame and low self-worth: as long as everything looks perfect, you don't feel bad about yourself.

People-pleasing

It's fine to want to please someone you care about, but codependence means you don't feel like you have a choice. You change yourself in order to be more lovable to the other, making big efforts to be what you imagine they to want you to be.

Saying no is difficult if you are codependent. You tell yourself you don't want to hurt their feelings, and you will go out of your way and sacrifice your own needs to accommodate others, often not getting as much in return. This can leave you feeling used or taken advantage of.

Poor boundaries

Boundaries are sort of an imaginary line between you and others. It divides up what's yours and somebody else's, applying to your body, money and belongings, as well as your feelings, thoughts and needs.

Codependence means having blurry or weak boundaries, feeling responsible for other people's feelings and problems, or blaming your own on someone else.

Sometimes it means having rigid boundaries that are more like walls. Within these walls you are closed off and withdrawn, making it hard for anyone to get close to you. It is not uncommon to flip back and forth between having weak boundaries and having rigid ones.

Dysfunctional communication

Having a hard time communicating our thoughts, feelings and needs is linked to poor boundaries and is sometimes a result of not actually *knowing* what we think, feel or need.

Other times we know, but won't own up to it. We're afraid to be honest, because we don't want to look bad, or be judged, or upset someone else.

Instead of saying honestly, 'I don't like that,' we might pretend that it's okay, tell someone what to do, or vent to a third person.

Perhaps we even stop communicating altogether to avoid uncomfortable conversations or conflict. When we try to manipulate the other person or manage their thoughts, feelings or perceptions, communication becomes dishonest and confusing.

Reactivity

As a consequence of poor boundaries we react to everyone's thoughts and feelings. If someone says something we disagree with, we either believe it or become defensive. Because there is no boundary, we absorb their words and take their opinions too personally.

With a clear boundary, we'd realize it was just their opinion and not a reflection of us, and would not feel as threatened by disagreements.

Caretaking

Another effect of poor boundaries is wanting to help and solve other people's problems for them, sometimes to the point of giving yourself up. It's natural to feel empathy, but putting other people ahead of yourself and needing to be needed or to 'fix' people is a form of codependence. You might even feel rejected if the other person doesn't want help.

Initially the term codependent was used to describe the nature of the relationship between an alcoholic or other addict and their partner or family member ('the enabler').

Control

Control helps codependents feel safe and secure. Everyone needs some control over events in their life, but codependent, unhealthy control limits the ability to take risks and share feelings. Addictions may develop to help loosen up, or hold feelings down.

Codependents also need other people to behave in a certain way to feel okay and hence need to control those around them. In fact, people-pleasing and caretaking can be subtle ways to control and manipulate others.

Alternatively, codependents may be bossy and tell others what they should or shouldn't do, think or feel. This is a violation of someone else's boundary.

Obsessions

As a result of dependency, anxieties and fears, codependents have a tendency to constantly think about other people or relationships. They can also become obsessed when they think they've made or might make a 'mistake'. They may lapse into fantasy about how they'd like things to be, or about someone they love as a way of avoiding the pain of the present.

Denial

Denial often means we think that the problem is someone else or the situation. We either complain about or try to fix the other person, or go from one relationship or job to another, not owning up to the fact that the problem is ours.

As codependents we deny our feelings and needs. It means we don't know what we are feeling and are instead focused on what others are feeling. The same thing goes for our needs. We pay attention to other people's needs and not our own.

Although some codependents seem needy, others act like they're self-sufficient when it comes to needing or accepting help. They won't reach out, and they have trouble receiving. They are in denial of their vulnerability and need for love and intimacy.

Problems with intimacy

This doesn't necessarily mean sex – although sexual issues can be a reflection of an intimacy problem – but opening up to someone in an intimate relationship. Because of the shame and weak boundaries, you might fear that you'll be judged, rejected, or left.

On the other hand, you may fear being smothered and losing your autonomy; hence avoiding getting too close to people at all cost. Often these opposites go together in a codependent relationship.

Dependency

Codependence means you need other people to like, respect or approve of you to feel okay about yourself. You're afraid of being rejected or abandoned.

You may *need* to be in a relationship, because you feel depressed or lonely when you're by yourself. This makes it hard to end a relationship, even when it is a painful or abusive one. As a result you may end up feeling trapped. Your intimate relationships may have repeating patterns of love addiction and love avoidance.

Black and white thinking

Codependents tend to think and react in extremes. In their world things are all or nothing. If their partner asks for some space, a codependent will avoid him for days. If they receive criticism in a relationship or at work, a codependent may think it's best to end it there, or mull over it for ages, feeling terrible.

They tend to either give all (= give too much) or close down and give nothing, maybe alternating between the two. This results in drama and lack of balance in relationships.

Painful emotions and emotional suffering

Codependency creates stress and leads to many painful emotions. Shame and low self-esteem create anxiety and fear about being judged, rejected or abandoned, making mistakes, being a failure, feeling trapped by being close, or being alone.

Other symptoms lead to feelings of anger and resentment, depression, hopelessness, and despair.

Everyone feels emotional pain from time to time, but codependents turn pain into suffering; its dramatized form. When the feelings are too much, they can feel numb.

How to break it

Remember that it always takes two to have a codependent relationship! Simply recognizing and becoming aware of these unhealthy patterns within us is the first huge step toward changing them and becoming free.

Working on our self-love and boundaries is essential in breaking codependence. More can be found on these topics in these chapters: 'Self-love and what it looks like in action' and 'Creating healthy boundaries'.

> ### Facing codependence
>
> Pia Mellody's book 'Facing Codependence' is an international bestseller and a highly regarded self-help book that shows us how to break the binds of codependence, have intimate relationships without losing ourselves – and feel whole again.
>
> It is the backbone of countless successful therapy and recovery programs all over the world, and I recommend it to all my clients as well as anyone reading this book.

A codependent person is one who has let another person's
behavior affect him or her and who is obsessed with controlling
that person's behavior.[16]
Melody Beattie

'Same, same, but different'

How to embrace the differences in relationships and move from conditional to unconditional love.

Intellectually it is easy to understand and accept that we are all unique and special individuals. Even if we surround ourselves with people who are more like us; have similar values, interests and lifestyle, there will always be things we don't see or experience the same way. There is simply no escaping this simple fact of life: we won't always agree.

So let's be honest, sometimes it is frustrating how different we are. Particularly in intimate relationships, the differences and variety in individual perception are the cause of a lot of conflict. Or, to be more exact, rather than the differences themselves, it is our *intolerance* of them that causes problems. We interpret them to mean that one of us must be wrong and the other right, that they mean we are not understood – or take them as evidence to show that we are not suitable for each other, let alone soul mates, after all.

KNOWING YOURSELF THOROUGHLY

The more confident you are in yourself and the more you accept your own personal reality, the less threatened and triggered you are by other people's different views, perceptions and feelings. In other words, where you feel triggered by the views or opinions of others, there is likely to be something you are not accepting, confident about, or at peace with in your reality. Topics such as politics, religion and parenting are common triggers!

However, it perhaps deserves a mention that the true *inner* confidence we are talking about can look very different from the external *air* of confidence, which in some cases is but a façade covering up hidden insecurity.

Needing to have power over others and call the shots is usually driven by fear and distrust, out of which we feel the need to control everything and everyone around us; otherwise we would feel unsafe.

So each time you notice yourself getting fired up, insulted, hurt or annoyed by somebody else's view which differs from yours, or feel the need to argue your point to get them to agree, you can do a little inner investigation to find out what actually has been triggered:

- Does it make you feel unsafe?
- Does it make you feel less-than?
- Does it feel unfair?
- Does it make you feel judged or misunderstood?

What do you judge them as?

Here's a simple example

Perhaps it annoys you that your partner wants to spend more private time with his friends without you (or vice versa!). You would be happy to spend all that time together, with friends and partners combined. You are tempted to make him wrong in your head and even out loud. Or it makes you feel hurt but you don't want to say anything.

Either way, it has triggered a reaction in you. But what is it really about? How does it make you feel? Rejected? Scared that he doesn't love or want you as much as you want him? Angry that he can have what he wants (time with friends) and you can't (more time with him)?

Be as honest and candid as you can with your answers. Remember it is not about them but about how you actually feel – it's not a question of right or wrong, justified or unjustified.

Most of the time simply owning, sitting with and perhaps expressing how you feel is enough to discharge the trigger. Suddenly you become aware of what is really going on and what it is about rather than reacting unconsciously like puppets, making each other wrong.

Questions to help the self-inquiry

- When someone doesn't see things the same way you do, does it bother you or do you make them wrong in your mind?
- When your partner or friend has a different view on something you are talking about, do you end up arguing to make him see your point or to admit that you are right? Or do you feel the need to agree with her so that she doesn't judge you or make you wrong for having a different opinion?
- Are you able to have conversations where you acknowledge and accept the fact that you have different views but remain curious about the other's opinion, wanting to genuinely understand it?

GIVING UP THE BATTLE

Trying to decide who is right and who is wrong is the one debate we can never get fully satisfactory answers to and, even if we did, it wouldn't serve any purpose other than boosting our ego. Nobody likes being made wrong for our feelings, desires, thoughts or experience.

What we can do is share our reality, our perceptions and feelings with others, without trying to change theirs. (For those of us who have spent our lives defining our views of right and wrong, categorizing things as good or bad, acceptable or unacceptable, managing people's views and opinions of us and the world, this may be hard at first.) This is real intimacy. When we do this, our relationships will never get boring.

We will never stop learning about each other or ourselves, and our relationships will be ever evolving.

Respecting our different, relative realities, the way we experience and interpret the world around us, and sharing our experience without trying to change the other's is the main practice to build more unconditional love and intimacy in our life.

It doesn't mean that you like or love your partner or friend as long as he thinks the way you do, behaves the way you want, agrees with you on everything, and feels the same way (or else you will withhold your love).

It means that you love him *because* you do all that differently. You love him *because* he challenges you and because, through him, you see things in ways you never would just on your own. That is unconditional love, the key to successful, healthy and easy relationships.

The ideal of unconditional love mustn't be confused with codependence. It shouldn't be used as an excuse to fail to communicate boundaries or put up with abuse. Loving someone doesn't mean that you have to be with them. It's worth figuring out what kind of things are dealbreakers for you in intimate relationships.

Unconditional love is a big call; so don't beat yourself up when you fall short of it – we all do! However, bit by bit, with practice, you can expand your capacity to love and accept others – and yourself – for who they are.

Your ability to love another is infinitely entwined with your level of self-love. Work on it and all of the above will fall into place!

It is not our differences that divide us. It is our inability to recognize, accept and celebrate those differences.[17]
Audre Lorde

Playing by the rules

Setting rules of the game in relationships. Who decides what's okay and what's not?

There comes a time in every relationship when we realize that in certain areas of our shared path our boundaries differ. What is totally cool and acceptable for one, doesn't go down so well with the other. He thinks watching online pornography is fine, and she thinks it is borderline infidelity.

Particularly in romantic relationships and the ones where we are deeply emotionally involved, we often interpret conflicting views and boundaries in complicated ways. We take them personally, make each other wrong, or try to change each other.

But there is no universal book of rules that tells what's right or wrong in relationships. So how do we decide what's okay and what isn't?

Do you discuss your relationship drama with friends, asking for their opinion on what kind of behavior is acceptable and what isn't?

Do you look to your friends to affirm your opinions or to confirm that your partner's / boss's / other friend's viewpoint is wrong?

Do you give others relationship advice based on what you believe is right, what can work and what can't?

The battle of right and wrong

When one person does something the other is triggered by or doesn't like, the tendency is to spend time analyzing and arguing over who is right and who is wrong – sometimes even analyzing who has the 'right' to feel angry, hurt, upset, etc. The opinions are normally not based on anything other than ideas in our head justifying how we feel.

We may discuss the issue with friends over and over, asking for their opinions, trying to decide our stand and to gather evidence to back it up. The internet is full of chat rooms and Facebook groups with ongoing heated discussions on all possible relationship issues such as cheating, privacy, honesty, sex, pornography, as if they – or anybody – could give us the answers!

The battle of right and wrong is hopeless and can often continue a disproportionately long time.

So what should the rules or boundaries be based upon – on what our culture or society says is 'right', what our friends think is acceptable, or something else?

At the end of the day the only people whose opinions and feelings really matter are the two (or more) actually *in* the relationship. In most situations they are the only ones whom the subject affects in any way, no matter how strong a view others might have.

The more we let go of all *shoulds* and black and white thinking, the more we can actually be true to ourselves and our feelings – and stay open, vulnerable and real with each other.

Open communication

In each relationship the rules are for us to make and negotiate, together. Hence open communication is needed to establish what is okay and what's not for each individual. Doing this ahead of time can save us from a lot of pain and anguish, but of course we don't always know where the differences lie before they emerge.

Conscious communication requires that we actually listen to each other and stay open to hearing their different ideas without blaming or arguing our point.

When we feel made wrong most of us automatically defend ourselves, and when we are on the defense it's not so easy to stay open and vulnerable. We might close off or strike back, and before we know it, there they are; our two defenses doing their dance, which normally doesn't lead to fruitful results.

Usually when we feel the need to argue it is because our feelings are hurt or we are feeling insecure and we are trying to protect ourselves. Expressing this is a good start. It opens up the conversation in a way that provokes the most honesty and least defensiveness.

Open communication isn't always going to be clean, tidy and calm. We won't always be able to communicate in the most conscious, clear manner. Sometimes it is going to be messy and intense. It's okay!

Heart to heart

When you feel the need to justify and find supporting evidence to back your case you are approaching the situation from your head, and rational mind. However what lies deeper than this are your emotions and how you honestly *feel* about the subject; the non-logical part. When you can get to this and own your feelings, first on a personal level, you are entering the heart.

Communicating directly from the heart and your feelings, as confronting as it may be to begin with, you have a much better chance of an open, loving and respectful exchange where both parties feel heard.

Letting go of the external backup and evidence, and basing our rules and boundaries on our own values and morals and what feels right for the people *in the relationship* ensures the best outcome (and least headache and hurt in the future).

Of course what feels right may be different for each side; so some loving negotiation may be in order. It is quite possible that there are topics we simply can't come to an agreement on. Then it is a matter of deciding whether it is fundamental or not, whether it is a difference we can live with and embrace, or if it makes our life together impossible.

However when we approach the conversation from a vulnerable, open place we are most often happy to meet each other somewhere in the middle.

Changing the rules

It is not uncommon for we humans to resist change. Change can be experienced as something scary or threatening if we interpret change to mean that our relationship or the love we feel for each other is in danger.

We may go to colossal efforts to fit into the expectations of the other based on the past, or keep our partner from growing in fear that they may grow past us and leave us behind.

However change is the one thing we definitely can rely on in life. Everything alive is ever evolving and growing, no matter what. As a result of our personal evolution our relationships will change, no matter how we may try to resist it. The more we can welcome this change and allow it to take place, the happier and more content we are in our relationships.

This also means that the rules may need to change over time. What was okay with us before may not work for us anymore. Or as we become more comfortable and secure with each other, we may find that the things that bothered us before no longer bother or threaten us. Therefore the rules between us can be negotiated and re-negotiated.

The only universal rule is that there are no rules. There is only what we are, and are not, okay with. That is the only thing that matters; not the opinions, beliefs or judgments of others, not our culture's unspoken moral code – just us and what we need to feel safe, loved and respected in our relationships.

There is no universal book of rules that tells us what is and what isn't okay in relationships. It is for us to figure out together.
Liisa Halme

What is true self-love and what does it look like in action?

There is only one person you have to live with for the rest of your life. Having a loving relationship with that individual is of utmost importance to your happiness. It is the one relationship that will affect all the rest: that with yourself.

I used to think that my external air of confidence and my inflated self-esteem (read: superiority complex) meant that I loved myself. I also used to think that other people were the source of problems in my relationships and life in general.

I both chuckle and shudder thinking about that, because it couldn't have been further from the truth! The reality was that I actually had a very narrow idea of how I, or other people, 'should' be, act or behave, which meant that my love for myself as well as others was very conditional.

I was a perfectionist who felt blinding shame whenever I made a mistake – even if I covered it up from everyone including myself – and who was super sensitive to criticism because I was overly critical of myself. Now this is about as far from self-love as one can get.

I found out the hard way that learning to love myself wasn't about trying to be perfect or good enough (to deserve love), or even about thinking highly of myself. It was actually a journey of exploring my darkness; all of those parts of me that I had denied, disowned or been ashamed of. Only through discovering and learning to accept those parts of me that I *wasn't* proud of did it become possible to love myself more fully and less conditionally.

Loving yourself and others

Your capacity to love yourself will always be reflected in your relationships with others. In other words, the more fully you can love yourself the greater your capacity to love another and to receive love, which makes it the perfect place to start if you want to create more love in your life! (Who doesn't?!)

If you don't feel completely loved and supported by the universe at all times, chances are that you have some work to do on your level of self-love. You could have some unconscious beliefs against giving yourself all that you want, letting love and support in, and feeling fantastically good about yourself.

Your level of self-love doesn't only affect your relationships but it affects every single aspect of your life, from your health, wealth and success to your happiness and how you feel inside.

In learning to love yourself more fully it is helpful to look at where you are *not* treating yourself as lovingly as you could.

A few questions

- Do you find it hard or uncomfortable to accept compliments, gifts or loving acts of service from others?
- Do you have the habit of always putting others' needs ahead of your own?
- Do you feel depleted and drained in relationships, like you're not receiving as much as you give?

- Do you feel obligated to please others at the expense of your own boundaries?
- Do you often say yes because you think you should, when really you want to say no?
- Are you scared or hesitant to ask for what you need at work or in relationships?
- Are you frequently critical of yourself *or* others?
- Do you frequently feel annoyed or disappointed with other people?
- Do you often end up in unfulfilling relationships?
- Do you make others wrong in your head and think they should be more like this or that (or more like you)?
- Do you tend to eat, rest and exercise as a means to feel *good enough,* or to punish or reward yourself? (Here's a hint: If the word 'deserve' is in your thoughts about food or exercise, then it is about punishing or rewarding. For example: 'I went for a run this morning – so I deserve to eat this piece of cake or chocolate.')
- Do you often feel like the world isn't giving you as much as you deserve?
- When things start going your way – when you land your dream job, relationship or house – do you feel bad or guilty or ashamed about telling others?

All the 'yes' answers are indications of where you aren't loving yourself as much as you could, where you aren't letting love in, or where you are projecting your lack of self-love onto others.

'Love your neighbor as yourself'[18]

The Bible instructs us to love our neighbor *as we love ourselves.* It doesn't tell us we should always put others' needs ahead of our own, or sacrifice our happiness, health and well-being in the name of serving others. No: it gives us permission to love ourselves at equal measure to the love we give each other, no more, no less. This is realistic!

What makes you feel loved?

It can be interesting and fruitful to investigate what self-love really means to you, and how you show it in real life actions.

We all express and need love to be shown to us in individual ways: we have different 'love languages'.[19]

The thing that we most desire or need from others – our friends, family or partner – is almost always the thing we are not providing for ourselves. Whether it is respect, quality time, emotional support, honesty, having faith in ourselves, or something else, it is a good indication of what we need to give ourselves more of.

What is it *specifically* that makes you feel loved?

Is it time and presence, acts of service, words of affirmation, physical touch and affection, or gifts?

SOME OF THE GREATEST ACTS OF SELF-LOVE

Forgiveness

When you truly forgive someone and take personal responsibility for your emotions and experience, you release yourself from the hold and bind of other people's thoughts, emotions and actions.

This includes forgiving yourself and accepting all your emotions. Before you can fully forgive anyone, you need to get clear about *what* you are forgiving: the event *as well as all of your emotions around it.*

By skipping over this step you are able to forgive only partially; thus to have the unowned emotions bite you on the bum later on!

Honoring your personal reality, communicating healthy boundaries and asking for your needs to be met

Learning to honor your own truth (your personal experience, your emotions, thoughts and beliefs) and breaking patterns of codependence by communicating that personal reality – as well boundaries that feel right for you – means that you stay in your personal power; safe and protected.

Each time you communicate your boundaries you are respecting your truth. This could mean learning to say no when you want to say no, rather than the reluctant yes when you aren't able to give a true, wholehearted one.

Another vital way of doing this is asking for your needs to be met. 'Ask and it will be given to you…'[20] is another famous Bible quote – wise words.

The above great acts of self-love also lead to greater intimacy with others.

Exercising your freedom to choose and dropping the shoulds

Remembering that you have a choice means you can let go of many things that cause you misery and instead give yourself what makes you happy. The simple act of doing more of the things you love brings more pleasure and joy into your life.

Each time you think, 'I should be more like this or that', or, 'I should do this or that', you can stop and ask, 'Do I really want to?'

Most of your *shoulds* come from your thinking you ought to do, or be, something other than what you are in this moment. Many of these beliefs originate from somewhere outside of yourself: your family, culture, peers, religion, media etc.

When, instead, you ask, 'Do I really have to / want to?', you are making a conscious choice to stay true to yourself. It also reduces the feelings of resentment that grow when you do something reluctantly, just because you or someone else thinks that you should.

Acting on your dreams

The Bible verse continues: 'Seek, and you will find. Knock, and it will be opened for you.'[21] By taking action towards manifesting your dreams into reality you tell yourself and the universe that you are worth it. (Picture the flick of the amazing head of hair...)

It is okay if your dreams change along the way. You may even find out that your dreams weren't yours to begin with, and that your true life purpose and calling lies somewhere new and unexpected. But taking action tells both your own subconscious mind, and the world, that you are serious about your dreams; not just passively wishing!

Letting go of shame or unhealthy pride

Unhealthy or false pride – the kind that can be hurt – is actually a coverup or a protection against shame. In other words, when our pride is 'hurt', what we actually feel is shame.

Shame is the opposite of self-love, because shame says, 'There is something wrong with me / I am not enough'. Unfortunately we can't reason our way out of shame, much like we can't reason our way out of any emotion – we can merely cover it up and make it unconscious.

The only way to truly move past it is being willing to feel it first. Paradoxically the way to sincere self-love often goes through acknowledging and accepting our shame and self-hate!

Investing in our health, high quality food, body-mind treatments and emotional education

Most of us spend a fair bit of money on clothes, shoes and the way we look. Of course we can genuinely enjoy that too, but it's not very often that we spend time at home alone dressed in our most beautiful outfit just to enjoy how it feels.

We may tell ourselves that we are loving ourselves by going to the gym, working out and watching what we eat, but whether it is loving or not depends on what drives our 'health-consciousness'.

Are you exercising, eating, resting and indulging as a way to feel better about yourself, to feel good enough – to punish or reward yourself? How do you feel if you slip from your regime? Is it really driven by love, or by fear?

When you do things out of fear you will feel bad, guilty or ashamed if you fail to meet your expectation (say, go to the gym three times every week or eat no carbs at night).

The difference is that when you do something out of love it is always enjoyable. There is no element of *should* or deprivation in it. It is out of freewill and desire, rather than guilt or obligation.

Investing money into how you feel inside and out, you are literally valuing yourself. It is powerful and integrated self-love in action.

The more you get used to loving yourself freely and wholly without guilt or shame, the more love you will experience in your life as it is reflected back to you through people and the world around you. It is also the best gift you can give to other people in your life!

Lack of self-love is the most critical thing standing in the way of our dreams.
Liisa Halme

Heal the inner child

Connecting with your inner child brings a whole new perspective to your healing process: it allows you to give yourself what you missed out on as a child, love yourself the way you needed to be loved, as well as step into the shoes of the mature adult who has freedom of choice.

As you have probably figured out, a lot of your subconscious conditioning and emotional baggage come from childhood – yes, even if you had one of those happy 'Disneyland childhoods' where the sun always shone and every day was a birthday. Regardless of what your childhood was like or what kind of memory you have of it, what has happened has happened; no amount of inner work will change the past or erase events from your history and it may seem hopeless to try and alter things that are already embedded in your psyche. So what to do? What's the best way to go about it?

INTRODUCING THE 'INNER CHILD'

The concept of the inner child is widely recognized in psychology and psychotherapy. The inner child is the child you once were, an aspect of you that is still young and childlike, with childlike qualities and childish responses to events. Your inner child can be joyful, enthusiastic, playful and innocent. But it can also be needy, self-centred, irresponsible and have temper tantrums, just like a real kid. When you get emotionally triggered it is usually your inner child popping out for an unexpected visit! The inner child holds all the unresolved childhood hurts and traumas that still affect your life today. This is why working with your inner child has unparalleled benefits to your healing process in the later years too.

Immature child in an adult body

The fact is, if we are lucky enough to stay alive, we all grow older. But this doesn't always mean that we psychologically or emotionally grow up and become adults.

True adulthood means acknowledging, accepting, loving and parenting our inner child, filling our own needs, looking after ourselves and so on. For many of us this never happens: in an attempt to grow up we merely learn to shut down our playfulness, innocence, sensitivity, wonder and all those positive childlike qualities that we consciously or unconsciously don't approve of in adulthood.

Our unprocessed traumas and unresolved emotions from childhood still resurface decades later each time they are triggered, quite possibly multiple times every day! The immature child inside of us unconsciously directs our life with her juvenile, immature reactions. She makes important adult decisions for us, tries to have an independent life, a career, mature relationships and so on.

You guessed it: the result is a train wreck. No wonder our relationships are a mess and we end up making bad decisions for ourselves. It's also no wonder that we feel so anxious, afraid, insecure, inferior, small, lost, or lonely. Think about it: how else would a child feel having to fend for herself in an apparently adult world without proper parental supervision, protection, structure or support?

The downfalls of pseudo-adulthood

When we approach our healing process from the pseudo-adult mind we are likely to merely build more sophisticated defense systems rather than achieve actual deep healing. We learn to rationalise our feelings away, minimise our traumas, think positively, rise above, toughen up, not give a f**k, gloss over, or just forget. In other words we treat ourselves the way we were treated as a child.

As pseudo grown-ups we tend to be incredibly hard on ourselves. We can treat ourselves harshly, have unrealistic demands, neglect our own feelings and not give ourselves what we want and dream of – and that's just for starters.

So why is it that so many of us look for validation from the outside? Why don't we provide for our own emotional needs?

The simple answer is that when we didn't have our needs met as a child, we didn't learn how to do it for ourselves. We didn't completely step into the shoes of the adult, but in some ways stayed a child who reacts like a child and needs looking after. We therefore desperately need people (partner/boss/parents/friends) to approve of us, to agree with us, to give us love so that we can feel okay.

How does connecting with your childhood self change your life today?

When you step into the shoes of the wounded child you once were – and connect with him, his feelings, needs and dreams – something magical happens: that child, that still tender part of you, suddenly feels seen and heard, even accepted, protected and loved.

He starts to feel safe and welcome as he is no longer shut into some dark, forgotten corner of your unconscious mind. And as the child begins to feel safe, he actually begins to grow up and mature.

Imagine this

- How much more forgiving would you be with your own child than you are with yourself?
- How much more love would you feel for her?
- How protective would you feel towards her?
- How much of your time and energy would you give her?

When you begin to connect with the child you once were – even think of her as your *own* child – it becomes much easier to find softness and tenderness towards her. Loving and accepting your inner child with all her needs, wants and feelings translates into true self-love, the most important ingredient for emotional healing (not to mention healthy relationships).

Entering true adulthood

The transformational part is that now, as a grown-up, you can parent yourself. This means you can be both the parent and the child at the same time. You can give the child part of you what she needs; value her, believe in her, protect her, let her play. You can start to fill your own love needs that weren't met early on and stop looking for someone else to do it for you.

As the adult you have the power to provide for yourself, not just financially but also emotionally. You are no longer dependent on somebody else to make you feel safe, loved and accepted.

(Of course I am not saying that as adults we no longer need other people. But when we learn to love and nurture ourselves we will soon begin to receive more love and nurturing from each other as well. Maybe it was there all along and we just become more open to letting it in!)

Here's the only catch: building a strong foundation for any relationship takes time and commitment. In much the same way, working with the inner child is a long-term process. We can't expect that the child within us, who has been abandoned for decades, is going to trust us fully after a quick 15-minute exercise. In fact they might be quite untrusting of the adult self to start with. Rightly so. Stay persistent!

PRACTICE: CONNECT WITH YOUR INNER CHILD

Find a time and place where you can be comfortable and undisturbed for a while. If you have a childhood teddy, doll or cuddly toy, take that with you. Otherwise a pillow will do. Bring a pen (or ideally two different colored pens) and paper.

As always, begin the exercise by taking in a nice deep breath, then let it all out without any force, like a sigh. Repeat a few more times until you feel yourself beginning to relax. Bring your awareness to your body and breath and how they feel.

Imagine that there is a young child in front of you, a child that depends on you. If you are a woman, then it is a girl, if you are a man then it is a little boy. Imagine him at a young age, well under 10 years. He is your child. As you look at him closely you notice that he is actually a young version of yourself.

Study his face: What's his expression like? What is he feeling? How does it feel to be him?

Tell him out loud: 'I'm here now. I'm with you now.'

How does he respond? What does he say?

Begin a dialogue on paper. Your dominant hand writes as your current self and your non-dominant hand writes as your childhood self. Ask the child how he is feeling, what he needs, what he wants and what he is afraid of. Another powerful question is: What do you need from me in order to feel safe?

The inner child may respond something along the lines of: 'I need you to take better care of your finances' or 'I need you to leave that abusive relationship' or 'I need you to take better care of your health'. Let the dialogue flow without too much thinking.

Remember that in order for that trusting relationship to build between the child and the adult self, you need to honor the promises you make to your inner child. So only make promises you can keep. It is a two-way conversation, and simply hearing your inner child out will have a huge impact. You will be amazed to see the results afterwards.

If it feels hard to get started with the exercise, you may want to have some pleasant classical or instrumental music playing in the background. Make sure your breath keeps flowing freely. Perhaps let yourself have a little dance or a wiggle to the music to get out of your head and into your body, and get into a flow (alpha) state.

Keep writing the dialogue until you feel a softening or an opening take place, or have an actual emotional release. Tears may begin to flow (this is good!) and you may want to cuddle your teddy or pillow, holding him tight in your arms, like your child. You can even stroke his hair or sing to him; whatever you enjoyed or wanted done to you as a child.

If doing this exercise or reading this chapter feels very awkward to you, then take it as a sign that you are probably quite out of touch with your inner child. You may have shut him away and be reluctant to connect with him. This is okay too, but I urge you to at least keep the dialogue going and do it regularly until you feel more at ease together.

The child part of you is yearning for this. As bizarre as it may sound, this is incredibly healing. You have nothing to lose by giving it a go. What you can gain, though, is infinite. Reduced stress and anxiety for starters.

Caring for your inner child has a powerful and surprisingly quick result: Do it and the child heals.[22]
Martha Beck

Creating more love and intimate connection

Have you been looking for love in all the wrong places? Learn why learning to love yourself is the most important factor in intimacy.

For a lot of my life I craved and looked for that true love where I would always feel deep connection and understanding with my partner, where I would never feel alone, and where I would feel loved and accepted no matter what.

Little did I know that there was only one person in the world who could give that to me: me!

Most humans, independent of age, race or cultural background, want more love and intimacy in our lives.

We want to be loved and accepted for who we are, not just for the way we look, the clothes we wear, the accomplishments or money we make, or other attributes that we have used to make up our persona.

Unfortunately we are often our own worst enemies when it comes to love and intimacy.

Lost connection

All too often our lack of intimacy and connection with others is due to our reluctance to share ourselves authentically, always showing the side of ourselves we want others to see, hiding our vulnerability and the parts of ourselves that we think are less than perfect, in the fear of being judged or rejected.

What we end up showing of ourselves is really a mask, a façade, a defense, or an ideal of who we'd like to be or what we expect others to want us to be – or to find cool or lovable.

We end up feeling alone, isolated, misunderstood and disconnected, even if we have a thousand friends on Facebook and a busy social life. We are left craving for someone to see us for who we are and to love us without judgments and conditions. But it is highly likely that we are not even giving anyone a chance to do so.

It's no wonder we are unwilling to share of ourselves authentically if there is so much that we are unable to love and unwilling to accept about ourselves!

This is where self-love comes into play: no-one can actually *make you feel loved* unless you love yourself first.

This is why looking for an outside source of love alone will never be a lasting solution. It puts the burden of an unreasonable and unrealistic expectation on the other, who has no chance in the world to meet it in the long term.

Love and intimacy with others follows love and intimacy with yourself. What this would look like is coming out of hiding, doing deep inner work to really get to know the deeper parts of yourself – your unconscious fears and other emotional content – and learning to lovingly accept and own them all.

Wherever we feel stuck in our lives, we are unconscious

Where you become conscious you remember your ability to choose and become free.

(I know this is a bold statement that you might want to object to. But do read it again, and then go ahead and test it out!)

So if there is something that isn't working for you in your life, be it lack of love or intimacy, the chances are that you have some inner work to do, bringing that which is unconscious into consciousness. This is the journey to fully getting to know, and becoming intimate with, yourself in order to find the love that you are craving for – first within yourself.

Intimacy through knowing yourself

Only when we know ourselves thoroughly are we able to share ourselves authentically and be vulnerable with one another. Why? Because when we don't know ourselves fully, it is impossible to share what we don't know – then we are relating to each other mainly from our defense.

Without vulnerability and letting down our guard and our defenses (at a pace both parties are comfortable with), there is no intimacy. The best definition of intimacy I have heard is *'sharing our reality with another without trying to change theirs'*.

This recognizes that our realities – our inner experience, thoughts and feelings – are different and they don't have to match in order for us to be close and intimate with each other. It also implies sharing our reality without trying to convince the other that our opinion, philosophy or way of seeing and interpreting the world is the right one. It implies respect and curiosity for the other's individual experience, thoughts and feelings.

'Intimacy' that requires the other to think and feel the same way as us is codependent and very conditional. True intimacy requires respect for each other's boundaries – which is only possible when our personal boundaries are clearly communicated (for example, 'this isn't okay for me…') without making the other wrong.

Healthy boundaries allow us to become vulnerable and open with each other when we feel ready, without feeling unsafe or exposed in a way we are uncomfortable with. In reverse, respecting our partner's boundaries could mean not instantly spilling our guts on the table for them, but sharing of ourselves at a pace they are comfortable with.

The same applies to sexual intimacy. Communicating and respecting each other's boundaries cultivates trust and helps us feel infinitely safer to relax, let go and enjoy each other in a much deeper level of physical intimacy than we would with weak or blurry boundaries.

A basic healthy boundary in sexuality is: *It is up to me when, where, how and by whom I allow myself to be touched. The same is true for you.*

A SIMPLE BUT POWERFUL INTIMACY PRACTICE

One of the most powerful and challenging intimacy practices is simple eye-gazing. Sit with a close friend or a partner, close enough to touch each other but without actually touching. Simply look into each other's eyes without saying anything. Keep your breath relaxed and deep – notice any temptation to tense the body or face or control your breathing, and, as much as possible, allow yourself to relax, breathe and keep eye contact without interruption. (It is equally powerful to do this exercise by yourself, using a mirror!)

You can keep going for five to ten minutes, or even longer. After the eye-gazing you can share with each other anything that you have been sitting on, anything that you have been wanting to say but haven't, any truth that you have not spoken to each other.

Communicate in a non-blaming way taking responsibility for your own feelings. (Read more about communication in the chapter on *The art of conscious communication.*)

This practice is bound to bring more intimacy into your relationship, breaking walls of protection or things left unsaid that may have built a distance between you.

The opposite of loneliness is not togetherness; it's intimacy.[23]
Richard Bach

What are we actually fighting about?

Discover why arguments and fights aren't usually about what we think.

Healthy disagreements are a part of every normal relationship, but sometimes the arguments we have with family or significant others are out of proportion. Rationally we know it's not such a big deal, but it still hurts more than we think it should, or our reaction is bigger than the situation warrants.

How is it that something relatively minor can bug us so much that is has the potential to escalate into a hefty row or an issue to hold against each other for ages?

The thing is, our arguments aren't always about what they seem to be. Most of the time the obvious subject of the matter is merely a surface layer, a symptom or a manifestation of something deeper. The 'deeper' doesn't have to mean anything huge or dramatic; it just means that it is less obvious, something we aren't consciously aware of.

Given that our conscious mind covers only about 10% of our thoughts and feelings, it's not uncommon for us to react from the unconscious part (the remaining 90% or so) that is hidden from our conscious awareness.

A helpful way to uncover what you are actually reacting to is to ask yourself: 'How has it left me feeling?'

Without making it about the other person (i.e., 'I feel like he is an idiot' or 'I feel like he just doesn't care'), you take it back to yourself and to how you feel: 'I feel sad' – or angry, unloved, unappreciated, powerless, afraid, ashamed, etc.

When you are willing to own your emotional response without making it wrong or blaming it on other people, the charge tends to dissipate, dissolving a potential argument before it begins.

Instead of getting stuck in the conscious story part (the who did or said what, and whether it was right or wrong) and getting into the actual *feelings and emotions* around it, you are diving deeper into the core of the issue where it can be released.

Own your stuff

Getting clear about your emotional triggers, taking responsibility and owning up to your own stuff and looking beyond who's right and who's wrong are some of the important practices that allow you to relate to others in a healthier way.

Owning your emotions and reactions can be confronting, and it takes courage. If you keep blaming and making each other wrong, as tempting as it may be, you stay in a stalemate.

Making ourselves wrong isn't the answer either. Even if one side 'gives in' and takes the blame, resentment can build up over time, keeping the relationship out of balance. Each time we actually communicate honestly how we feel, we open our hearts a little bit more.

Example
You are waiting in a restaurant and your partner is late, again. You could have almost predicted it. You feel disappointed and annoyed. Half an hour later they arrive, flustered, apologizing.

If you just say it's fine (because you don't want to be the nagging partner), but internally hold it – and all the times they've been late before – against them for the rest of the evening, you are not being

Liisa Halme

completely authentic. This creates distance between you two. Perhaps you end up having an argument about something else completely unrelated.

Even if you are hesitant to mention what's really bothering you (either for fear of exposing the smallness and pettiness of the matter, or for the fear of opening a can of worms in the case of something more serious) and instead keep sitting on it, it will most likely eat you up inside and the emotional charge will be expressed one way or another, no matter how you try to conceal it.

Closing off or staying away from subjects that we find confronting is a sure way to isolate ourselves. So it's best just to get it out there! It's always okay to communicate our feelings. However often when attempting to do so, we end up making the other person wrong for what's happened, rather than owning how we actually feel about it.

Being blamed or accused most often triggers a defensive reaction: the perfect recipe for an argument.

Hence when communicating our feelings to others it is important to try not to make them wrong. It is easier said than done, but it helps to remember that *no-one has the power to make us feel anything.*

When we *own* how we feel, and communicate it, we are making ourselves vulnerable. This means our heart is open, and it is only from an open place that we can reconnect with each other. When we are defensive our hearts remains closed and protected, leaving little chance for a loving resolution.

Back to the example: without making any comments or judgments on whether he is right or wrong to be late, you can take it back to yourself and examine how you really feel. On the surface you feel annoyed and you blame him for being late. But if you dig deeper and find the gist of how it honestly left you feeling, you may find you feel hurt, and less important than his job.

You may take it as evidence that he doesn't love you as much, or whatever else you make it mean in your head. In short you feel *hurt, unimportant and unloved.*

Maybe it's not the first time you felt the same way, and each time it stings that little bit more. These are the deeper reasons why we react. The deepest ones tend to be more emotional, less rational.

But it's good to remember we all have the right to our feelings, no matter how our logical mind tries to make them wrong and explain them away. We also have the right to express our feelings and emotions, meaning that we don't always have to (pretend to) be cool, calm and collected!

Accepting, owning and communicating how we feel helps release the emotional charge, which means it doesn't stay hanging around. If not released, the charge will stay within us and will be likely to spark up again as soon as an appropriate trigger appears – which normally doesn't take that long.

This is how we end up having the same arguments again and again.

No matter how confronting it may be to speak up and say how we feel, it is worth it!

When we communicate from the heart, are clear about our boundaries and needs, and accept that our realities can be different without one being right and the other wrong, there usually isn't very much left to defend or argue against.

It is just a matter of sharing our reality with one another, speaking our truth, and staying open to hearing theirs.

We seldom learn much from someone with whom we agree.[24]
Mokokona Mokhonoana

A word on forgiveness

There must be dozens, if not hundreds of books written about the importance of forgiveness, and how forgiving sets us free. Today's spiritual industry presents forgiveness as some kind of a golden ticket to internal peace and harmonious relationships. Maybe it can be, but often it is not. This is why.

The way I used to understand forgiveness was pretty similar to how it is portrayed in the Bible, many children's stories and fairytales: Somebody does something 'bad' or 'wrong' that goes against God's will or hurts another person / other people. God or the others get very mad or sad. Perhaps a punishment is given to the perpetrator, or at the very least is threatened. As a result the wrongdoer repents and asks for forgiveness. God or the others forgive him and everyone lives happily ever after, having learnt an important lesson. Or have they?

In my life the storyline looked something like this: A friend or a boyfriend would betray me; lie or cheat or do something along those lines. I would feel really hurt. If they apologized I would say I forgave them, but if they didn't, or worse yet, lied about it, I would get angry or withhold my love from them for a while. Eventually they would realize that they might lose the relationship, confess and say how sorry they are. I would forgive them and we would remain friends / lovers. But somehow the events would still haunt us years later. I would find it hard to trust them. I would still not be completely free from the hurt, even though I felt like I had honestly forgiven the wrong they had done. Often the same or similar scenario would repeat again.

What's wrong with the picture described above? Why doesn't forgiveness always work quite like it ought to? Why do we keep feeling hurt / angry / mistreated even after we have forgiven something? In other words, why do we keep feeling like a victim?

Reality is never as black and white as it is in fairytales where one is in the wrong and the other is right, one is bad and the other good. In real life it usually takes two to tango, and to keep a dynamic going in a relationship – even when we have bags full of evidence of how we are the innocent party who has been wronged!

Forgiveness or a shortcut?

Sometimes forgiveness is used as a quick fix or a copout. We gloss over painful events and feelings with the band-aid of superficial 'forgiveness', just to make it all okay and not to have to think or talk about it again. It is a way of avoiding having to take responsibility or process our emotions. If we took personal responsibility, in many cases there would actually be nothing to forgive. We would realize that how we interpreted events and what we made other people's actions to mean isn't necessarily their truth. We would also take ownership of our emotions and know that nobody can make us feel anything. (To clarify, I am not talking about referring blame from somebody else to yourself. You can read more about personal responsibility in the relevant chapter.)

If we think we have forgiven something or someone, but we haven't truly owned the full extent of our painful emotions around the event and the person involved, we have only forgiven superficially. In order to *fully* forgive we must first *fully* own the painful emotions we feel – only then will we know what we are actually forgiving; not just what has been done to us but also the emotions that have been brought up.

Sometimes having pardoned someone for the wrong they have done us can actually give us a false sense of superiority – like we have the upper hand over them. We hold the forgiveness card close to our chest as the one last thing we could pull out and remind the other person of the horrible thing they did to us and that we forgave. It makes us better than them! They *owe* us! This, of course, is just a defense. It is a way to keep making the other person wrong and at the same time use forgiveness as a quick fix, a way to make it all fine and avoid feeling or admitting our pain.

Empowered vs. disempowered forgiveness

If we forgive someone for having done something really unacceptable, aren't we letting them off the hook? Aren't some things just simply unforgivable?

Forgiveness doesn't have to mean turning the other cheek or letting ourselves be used as a doormat. We don't need to let our boundaries be crossed again and again (or worse, have no boundaries at all). That just isn't sustainable in the long run. We will eventually be riddled with suppressed negative emotions that will cause havoc in our life, our relationships and / or our health.

Forgiving something or someone doesn't have to equal accepting the behavior. We need only to accept that is has happened and that we can't change it. But we can still learn from the experience! It is up to us to make our boundaries clearer or take other necessary steps to ensure that the same doesn't happen again. This is empowered forgiveness. It really has very little to do with the other person. It is something we do for ourselves, to set ourselves free so that we don't need to keep holding onto the past and carrying it around with us any more.

When trust is broken

Betrayal is one of the most painful things in any intimate relationship. When we find out we have been lied to it can be hard to know what to believe any more. Suddenly everything may seem like a lie. Can the relationship and intimacy be repaired?

Even if we forgive someone we don't necessarily have to trust them again. Trust comes with time and patience. Sometimes it can be repaired and sometimes not. If the other person sincerely repents and is willing to work together to heal the relationship, it is possible for the bond to become strong again. But there is one thing both parties need to let go of: the hope that the relationship will ever be the same again. It may over time even become better than it was before, but it will never be the same. After betrayal and forgiveness, the relationship, including trust and intimacy, has to be built from the ground up again in order for it to become solid. This takes time and persistence, but as long as both parties are willing, it can work.

Forgive yourself

As always, it is easiest to start by healing your relationship with yourself. In the process of self-discovery you can uncover many cringe-worthy patterns, defenses and behaviors that are not easy to look at. Shame and self-blame kick in. Eventually you need to find a way to accept who you have been in order to heal old wounds and become free of them. Once you have forgiven yourself for anything you might feel guilty or ashamed about, it will be a whole lot easier to extend that forgiveness to those who may have wronged or hurt you.

FIVE STEPS TO FORGIVING FULLY

Unfortunately we cannot always jump straight into full, sincere forgiveness. There are some steps that we usually need to go through first. Here are the most important ones:

- *Own your story* (your interpretation of what happened and what you made it mean).

- *Feel and own the full extent of your emotions.*
- *Take responsibility for the above.*
- *Communicate* the above, and hear the other person out too. Listen to their side of the story. Processing things together will help understand and forgive each other more fully. (This step obviously isn't always possible in person. But you can talk to those who have passed away too!)
- *Set and communicate boundaries* if needed. Sometimes we don't even know where our boundaries are until they have been crossed! Then it's up to us to speak out.
- *Let it go!* Accept what has happened and that you can't change it. This includes accepting that the relationship may have changed as a result. This step cannot be rushed.

After sincere and wholehearted forgiveness you should feel a significant relief, a sense of freedom and lightness. You can love the other person freely again, without holding back or holding it against them. If this doesn't happen or the pain returns, you may need to go back and repeat some of the steps. Forgiving fully is a process and a choice you need to make again and again.

Forgive and forget was created by those unwilling to take responsibility for their own actions. Forgive and learn darling… forgive and learn.
Natalie Gaul

How to heal a broken heart

Why it can sometimes take so long to get over someone, and how to speed up the process.

Most of us have experienced heartbreak at some point: that excruciating pain and a feeling of emptiness like nothing else is ever going to matter again. We can't do anything without its being there, and nothing seems to alleviate the nauseating feeling.

If you know what I am talking about you'll also know that most often it eventually eases off and finally goes away. But why does it sometimes take such a hell of a long time? How can we feel so completely broken, even after a relationship that lasted a relatively short period of time, while at other times, we get over someone relatively quickly, even if we have shared much more of a history together?

Pain that is out of proportion

Sometimes the heartbreak over a relationship can seem so out of proportion because we are actually simultaneously grieving over many past loves lost, all the way from our childhood.

Let me explain. There are times in our life when the pain of loss is simply too great to take. This could be a rejection by or loss of a parent, a break-up of a family when we were little, even the death of our first pet and best friend – any and all of the incidents where we have not let ourselves feel and express the full extent of our grief and sadness.

We may have unconsciously shut down our pain just to cope, and even wondered how we were off the hook so easily. This is how: the pain didn't actually go anywhere; it stayed buried until it got another outlet to be felt and expressed again.

Heartbreak provides an opportunity for this old, internalized grief to be triggered, brought to the surface and processed.

Besides the love or loves lost there is often yet another aspect to our grief – the broken dreams – the future that we attached to that particular relationship and imagined with this person, the possible realities that we allowed ourselves to live in our head as if they were already real.

This in itself is not a bad thing, but when we have invested all our dreams in one person alone, and that person is no longer willing to play the part, we feel like the whole dream is lost forever. It's like we've not just lost what we had but also all those things we *could* have had as well. Ouch! It's helpful to remember that, even if it feels that way for a while, it doesn't have to be the end of our dreams forever.

Why the drama?

We may be unconsciously unwilling to let go of the pain because it is the last thing that connects us to this person and the dreams we had. In some cases extensive drama is created over shared possessions, businesses, pets, or, in worse case scenario, over children, as a means to hold on to the last thread of connection with – or power over – the other, however painful and dysfunctional it may be.

Getting through it

When we are in pain our tendency is often to avoid the pain at all cost – party our heads off, over-indulge, work, shop or exercise in excess –

anything to numb the pain and distract us from it. But unfortunately these avoidance tactics just postpone and prolong the process.

The only way to get through the pain is to literally go through it. What this means in practice is to allow ourselves to feel the pain to its full extent, including the pains of the previous losses and hurts that have been triggered. It's not always obvious what they are; so we might need to do a bit of digging to get to them.

A good way to do this investigation is to stay with that actual feeling you have around the heartbreak. Just allow yourself to feel it in your body, without the story of who did or said what and what it means. Keep your breath deep and free. Then ask yourself:

- How has this left me feeling? (Find single word answers: unloved, unwanted, broken, betrayed and so on.)

- What does this feeling remind me of?

- When was the first time I felt something similar in my life?

Let the answers come from the subconscious mind rather than from the analytical, rational mind that is likely to keep covering up the original pain.

Once you have the answer, even if it doesn't make sense to you straight away, allow yourself to stay with the emotions around that older incident. Just feel it; all the pain, sadness and whatever is there, without getting caught up with the story.

Remind yourself that the meaning you give to the events, such as: I am not loved, I am not lovable, or I will never find love like this again, etc. is only in your head and may have nothing to do with the other person's reality. The fact that he or she wants different things doesn't mean anything about you. Your worth is ultimately not dependent on them and what they think or feel about you.

Sometimes sitting with the emotions means that we have to cry and grieve for a really long time. Crying is actually the body's own natural cleansing and healing mechanism; it's a way to let go of the resistance.

After a good, healing cry we normally feel better, our heart is more open and we are less defended; more authentic. After expressing and letting out our grief all our energies flow better – we are no longer holding on and staying stuck in the suffering and the story.

We are actually physically, emotionally and energetically releasing and letting it go. When we finally acknowledge and let go of the past as well as the fixed ideas of the future, we are opening ourselves to a new future with more love than we could have imagined.

A broken heart is an open heart.
Unknown

PART 3

The mind stuff

Story vs. reality – the stories we tell ourselves

How dropping the story can help us transform our life

A lot of the time what we believe to be the reality is actually a story. As a matter of fact it is our reality, until we realize it is just a story… Let me explain: we tend to think that reality is something fixed, something solid that is 'just the way it is', and we tend to presume that what we perceive is the one true reality.

However, when investigating how different people perceive or experience the same situation we notice that our realities are often very unalike, even if from the outside they look exactly the same. It leads us to the conclusion that our reality is always our *personal interpretation*.

This doesn't make it any less real, but it can help us understand that we have more choice over it than we generally think!

MY REALITY VS. YOUR REALITY – WHAT'S THE STORY?

What I call *the story* is everything that is interpretation – everything I don't know for an absolute fact to be true. Let's say my husband is late from work, again, and I am waiting for him in a restaurant. About 20 minutes after the agreed time I start getting annoyed and upset.

The reality is that he is 20 minutes late and I am feeling upset and annoyed – that is unarguably real.

What is actually making me feel much worse is the story I create around his being late: I make it mean in my head that his work is more important to him, that he doesn't care about me as much and that he takes me for granted.

That is the story I make up. I don't know for certain that it is true. In fact his reality may be that he just had something unexpected come up at work that he has to deal with and he is trying to make it as soon as he can. My story may have absolutely nothing to do with his reality. (Remember this is not about who is right and who is wrong; rather to differentiate the reality from the story and point out that our realities can differ.)

The story I make up is usually the biggest trigger. It's what makes me react. When I drop the story – what I make his being late mean in my head – I actually feel much better and stop taking it personally. Perhaps I just have a glass of champagne while I wait, enjoy the atmosphere and the music, have a read of the menu and chat to the waiter about the specials.

Without the story (in this case) I have nothing to feel so upset about. Of course I can communicate my feelings to him and set a boundary such as 'Next time, if you are going to be late, please let me know.'

Alternative good strategy in communication is to own our interpretation and start with 'The story I'm making up in my head is...' This way the story gets out in the open but the other person doesn't feel accused. Exposing our story usually makes is dissipate pretty quickly.

Of course there are times when we are going to be upset no matter what. Let's say we lose a loved one in an accident. Nothing will take the pain away. We can create a story around the events and our pain that says 'God is cruel' or 'the world is not safe' or 'I will never be able to love again' or something else. This would be normal. But when we realize that this is just a story we created and see it for what it is, we can actually be with the pain itself and begin the healing process.

The story of my life

The above was a small example of something much bigger. When we become aware of our stories in different situations we can begin to notice patterns and similarities.

Indeed we often interpret reality through our own personal filter that affects how we perceive and experience the world around us. This filter is related to 'the story of our life'. Perhaps we have a filter of being made wrong, or being betrayed, or being unloved, or the world's being a scary, unsafe place. Maybe through our filter we see everyone else as being wrong, not doing enough, not being smart enough.

We may create a life story of illness, hardship and lack of love, unfairness, all through our interpretation.

At first we may not be able to see our story. We may see it as the absolute truth, the way things are, and gather a lot of evidence to back it up. We may be reluctant to own our filter or see through our story because we take it to mean that we were wrong – and of course we'd rather be right.

This is why it can sometimes be hard to let go of our story. So we hang onto it for dear life, even if the story is a shitty one that doesn't serve us! This is how we stay stuck.

But owning our story isn't about shaming or making ourselves wrong for having believed it in the first place. It's about opening our eyes to see it for what it is, and seeing more possibilities.

Certain stories are widely believed and so culturally accepted that it can be very hard to see past them. As a personal example, when I was younger I had a few health problems: asthma, allergies and serious hormonal issues.

According to doctors I should have been on multiple prescription medication (inhalers, preventers containing steroids, antihistamines, hormone replacement therapy and so on) for the rest of my life, and there was no chance of ever being cured from these conditions. I believed them. I believed that indeed there was something wrong with me, and had a lot of (medical, scientific) evidence to back it up.

Over time, however, I overcame this belief and realized it was just a story I had bought. Long story short (pun intended!) I moved on from the old story and paradigm, and as a result no longer have asthma or hormonal problems. In fact, while writing this, I am expecting our second baby (conceived 100 percent naturally, with ease) – something that I was always told would not be possible without medical intervention, if then. I have not needed any prescription medication for years*. Not to mention leaving behind a story of betrayal and lack of love that was causing me a lot of emotional pain in relationships.

This is how convincing our stories can be; they actually shape our physical reality! In fact they *are* our reality until we decide otherwise.

(*Remember that this is just a personal example and by no means intended as advice for you to stop taking your medication without consulting your doctor.)

Stories and manifestation

Let me give you a very common and practical example of how the stories we create keep us from manifesting our dreams.

Let's say that deep down you'd love to have more money and be able to afford a more comfortable lifestyle, freedom to travel when and where you like, and the house of your dreams (honestly, who wouldn't?). But since you don't have that, you make a story in your head of why having money and the things you secretly desire would actually be a bad thing.

So when you see the sexy Aston Martin DBS sports car that you secretly love, the conversation in your head could go something like this: 'I wouldn't want to have such an expensive car! It would be so annoying if it got scratched or damaged. Plus what's the point of having such a fast car in the city where you can't drive fast anyway? It's actually ridiculous…'

Or maybe you'd love to have an intimate relationship, or kids and a family, but haven't been able to make that happen yet. So you make a story in your head about how having a partner or a family would actually be a pain in the butt, and how lucky you are not to have to answer to anyone.

It becomes obvious how the justifications (= excuses, reasons, defenses) we come up with in an attempt to make our own reality more bearable, and not to feel the pain around not living our dreams, are the very same ones that keep us from having the things we desire!

Yes, these very stories that keep us a million miles from where we'd like to be and the life we'd like to live. So the sooner we own them and go, 'Shit, actually I'd love to have a car like that! I would love to have an intimate partner / kids / the career of my dreams / …' – the sooner we open ourselves up to receiving them!

When we do this we actually open ourselves to feel and release the emotions around not having these things. Our painful feelings can also be great motivators! For example, when we own how unhappy we are in our relationship, job or other situation, we have enough of an urge to do something to change it. When we avoid our pain we often sign ourselves up for even more pain in the future by minimizing our needs and desires and not giving ourselves what we want.

PRACTICE RECOGNIZING AND DITCHING THE STORY

If you are not sure of what the story of your life is, just listen to yourself each time you either vent at someone else, or silently in your head:

- Do you complain a lot or talk about how things or people should be?
- Do you blame other people or your circumstance?
- Do you explain and make excuses (you may call them 'reasons')?
- Do you put yourself or others down?
- Do you appear superior and/or attempt to control other people?

Whatever it is, you'll notice a theme that can reveal a great deal. Try not to make yourself wrong for it, but just notice when it's there and simply drop it. Instead, bring your awareness to your body, let your breathing deepen, and pay attention to the emotions that are there – both the painful and the elevating:

- What keeps you stuck?
- Where do you contract your body?
- What gives you joy?
- What do you deeply desire?

This way the head-tripping stops and you open up to possibilities that were hidden behind the veil of the story.

Keep reminding yourself that you write the story, nobody else, and that you have the power to either keep it, or let it go and change it to a different one.

Feel the feelings and drop the story.[25]
Pema Chödrön

Understand your defenses

Why most of your so-called personality is really a defense, and how to break out of it to find out who you really are.

Without even realizing it I used to have this belief that, as long as everything about myself and my life looked good, that was all that mattered. I spent my life making sure that everything I did was impressive, and neither I myself nor others would find anything to criticize. I was always positive and found the right words to say to others.

The problem was that, in living this way and solely focused on being the person I thought I should and wanted to be, concentrating on the esthetics and how others might see me, I was abandoning who I really was and how I felt on the inside.

I was well in my thirties before I realized that what or how I feel actually matters, and that it doesn't need to be justified or backed up with convincing evidence or story, and that, in fact, I too was allowed to have all of my feelings.

How our defenses are born

When I was a child I was the emotional one of the family. But in my family of origin being emotional was paralleled to being weak or wrong; so I learnt to control and suppress my feelings, to live up in my head and shut off the feeling part of myself.

Some variation of this process happens to most of us as we grow up: we learn to lock up aspects of ourselves away into the shadow part of our psyche, and only show and cultivate those parts which we believe are okay and good.

Many of our emotions, particularly the painful ones, get hidden in the shadow. Over time we even forget the existence of these feelings, desires, needs and personalities, as if they are no longer a part of us. However this means only that they leave our conscious awareness and become unconscious.

In order to protect and cover up those parts that we have hidden away – our wounding, our core beliefs, our disowned emotions – and to fill our unmet needs, we create what are called our defenses. They are a form of self-deception. Some of them can work in our favor, at least initially, but most of them will eventually not.

Why? Because they are covering up the truth about how we feel, about who we really are, keeping us from being vulnerable. Hence they prevent us from connecting with other people, ourselves and our feelings authentically. They create problems in relationships and keep us from expressing our painful emotions and healing our trauma and wounding – thus keeping us stuck.

My defense against the fear of being criticized, made wrong and rejected, was to become perfect at everything, flawless and impressive, so that there would be nothing to criticize.

I managed this quite well and externally my life looked pretty great. But inside I was still fearful and over-sensitive to anything that I could interpret as criticism, and was certainly too terrified to expose any vulnerable parts of myself to anybody, leaving me feeling very alone, isolated and yearning for connection.

Deep down I didn't believe I was lovable unless I was flawless. I also learnt to earn love by being useful (the way I had earned my big sister's love when I was young). So I became what people needed me to be: I was the supporter and confidante and rock for other people, yet unable to let anyone in to support me, unable to let love in! In some practical ways my defense worked for me, but in very many other ways it didn't.

My fear of criticism also caused me to keep myself small: I didn't dare let my light shine as brightly as I knew it could, in the fear of being judged or ending up failing and humiliated. So I kept myself in a very tight place between being perfect, in order not to be criticized, and not shining so as to stand out or to be singled out – and shot down.

But of course I was unable to see any of this from behind the veil of the idealized self, and instead projected all my problems outside of myself: to partners, family, friends, circumstance and even cities I lived in.

THE MOST COMMON DEFENSE STRUCTURES
Do you recognize yourself in one or some of them?

They are based on the Reichian character types,[26] simplified and renamed to be more accessible and less offensive.

The 'looking good' (or 'perfectionist') defense

This is the one I have just been describing. This is the person who is a self-controlled perfectionist. They want to always say the right thing, wear the perfect clothes for the occasion, know and manage what people think of him / her, appear successful, happy, intelligent, have it all figured out. They tend to excel in everything they do.

They often had to grow up too fast and in childhood were very mature for their age. They might live in what I call a Disneyland reality where the past, including childhood, and family life is sugar-coated and perfect.

They are masters of self-deception and often firmly believe in their own defense, and how perfect everything is in their life, despite the fact that something just isn't working (relationship, health or otherwise); hence they can easily end up confused about why it's happening to them. The person with the looking good defense cannot stand being criticized, or feeling out of control and has difficulty owning their 'negative' feelings other than for a 'good' reason (which usually involves someone else being in the wrong).

They seem very confident on the outside. They are physically balanced and beautiful, successful and are often highly sexual – or have problems with sexual intimacy. They are highly dependent on the approval of others, although will not readily admit this! They like feeling 'better than', and have a (false) sense of superiority. It can be difficult to get close to a person with this defense.

The looking good defense comes from an underlying inferiority complex, which the apparent superiority is covering up. The driving emotions are fear and shame (or fear of being shamed), even though those emotions may be completely disowned and unconscious.

The underlying core beliefs running the defense are 'I'm not good enough', 'I am bad / wrong' (hence the obsessive attempt to be good and right!), and 'I have done something wrong'.

These people have often had their hearts broken and subsequently closed to avoid feeling the full extent of the grief and pain. They may mistake sex for love, or have relationships with one or the other (sex or love) and are prone to love and sex addiction. The flow of energy between the heart and the pelvis (sexual centre) is cut off.

The 'controller' defense

This is slightly different from the former (who is *self*-controlled). People with the controller defense feel the need to be in control or in charge of their environment and people around them. They can come across as very charming and charismatic but also superior, dominating or intimidating.

They are often highly successful, leaders of the world, be they religious or political leaders, CEOs or rockstars. They have an idealistic self-image and are the masters of manipulation and can easily transform themselves to be what (they perceive) people need or want them to be. They need to be right and have the upper hand, even if it's by figuring out what's wrong with the other person so that they can feel superior – often truly believing that they are.

They like knowing how things are or 'should be', and can be thrown off-centre by the unknown. They dislike not knowing things, not being able to fix things, or people disagreeing with them, and are often trying to fix others or tell them how to think and feel. They also have a hard time trusting anyone to do things right, whether it is at home or in the workplace.

The underlying emotions are fear and terror; being in control makes them feel safe. A common defense protecting other emotions is anger. Physically they tend to be top-heavy; big body-builder's chest, shoulders and upper body, tight pelvis and a healthy, glowing skin color, and piercing eyes with an intense gaze. They may be tall or have an energy that towers over you.

The controller defense is born out of betrayal and uncertainty; in a situation where either one parent praises them and the other puts them down, or one parent alternates between the two extremes, objectifies and idealizes the child without seeing them for who they are. The child then becomes confused and does not know what the truth is.

Hence, in order to regain a sense of security and control, grows the obsession to always know how things are, what the right way is and what the truth is.

They need to focus on satisfying real needs and letting go of false needs (for example the need to control others) and can benefit from sharing difficulties and faults with others in a group setting and practicing being vulnerable in a safe environment.

The 'helplessness' defense

This defense is the flipside of the first, the looking good defense (a person with the looking good defense almost always has a less obvious helplessness defense too – but not necessarily vice versa).

The person with the helplessness defense has an air of:

- love me
- protect me
- feel sorry for me

about them – or the opposite:

- I don't need anyone
- I'm independent.

They like to talk a lot, complain or tell their story over and over again, which often is one of victimhood and blame. They fill their need for love and support by getting people to help them, listen to them, sympathize with them, protect them and rescue them. They often have a soft, childlike and depleted energy.

People with this defense often lose their power to others and they don't like upsetting people or the status quo. They might have a submissive role in their relationships or work situations, get caught in between, or be apologetic for no good reason.

Sometimes this helplessness defense is an *indirect* one, where the person denies their own personal needs; they dedicate themselves to others, always putting others first, slowly depleting themselves of energy and resources (perhaps ending up sick, and eventually helpless).

Physically they often have a collapsed chest and poor posture, with depleted energy in especially the chest. Eyes have a pleading, puppy-like quality. They have a lot of deep sadness and unmet love needs form early on in life, but they also need to get in touch with their healthy anger which will give them the strength to come out of disempowerment and victimhood, stand up for themselves and ask for their needs to be met.

The 'out of body' defense

People with this defense structure are usually somewhat alternative and like to spend their time in nature, with animals, books, angels, spirits or fictitious characters, and frequently can be found working in the esoteric field or leading a spiritual life.

They are often connected to spiritual and cosmic energies and may escape to a world of their own, to spiritual realms or fantasy, finding it hard to stay grounded on earth. They have to work hard (and may struggle) to fill their physical needs and make a living due to underlying disconnection with the material world. This may also manifest as a belief that the material side of life is unimportant.

These people are often very psychic, intuitive and intellectual. They may even be spiritual teachers or healers. But they are usually ungrounded, which shows in their life circumstance: Their life may fall apart, lack committed path or be unintegrated – or they engage in extreme spiritual living.

They can have a lot of energy in the body, but it is frantic, scattered and un-anchored. There is little energy in the legs to connect them to the earth. Their energy can feel 'elsewhere', detached or disconnected, and the energy field can look fragmented or shattered. Eyes can have a blank stare; they may have difficulty holding eye contact and it can seem like they are just not fully here.

The underlying emotions of the out of body defense are rage, terror and not wanting to be here in this body and this world due to lack of safety in the very early years. Their emotions can be all over the place, up and down, and without a container.

Physically they are often thin and have pale or grayish complexion. A left / right side imbalance may be apparent.

People with the out of body defense need to do daily grounding in order to get back into their body and learn to build a container for their emotions, rather than splitting off. Building clear boundaries is also helpful.

The 'endurer' defense

A person with this defense is often a little heavier, smiley, polite, pleasant and very (or almost too) nice. But underneath the niceness and the smile is an assassin: get on their wrong side and they will still smile at you, and then give you a big 'fuck you' sign when you turn your back. In other words they can be quite passive-aggressive.

Externally they say yes but internally and energetically it's a no. They almost thrive on aggression from others and may get pleasure from making others angry at them, then remaining calm and triumphant. They take pride in how much pain they can take without falling apart. They can be bullied or harassed for years yet will not ask for help or stand up for themselves. Instead will hold it in the body – and hold it against the world. They push down and store the emotional energies in their physical body, hence the heaviness and over-charge of energy.

A person with this defense is often a hard worker, doesn't complain (in direct words) and doesn't like to show emotion. They may even enjoy staying stuck as a form of revenge.

The underlying emotions for this defense are anger and shame.

Physically they are thick, compact, heavy (particularly lower half) and muscular. The face is often smiley and round.

They are grounded in the lower chakras and will benefit from learning to say no (rather than just thinking it), creative movement and self-expression, work on the upper chakras and connecting to spiritual life.

THE MANY WAYS WE ESCAPE – MOST COMMON DEFENSE MECHANISMS

Denial

This is the most classic of all defenses and one that goes together with many of the others. It's where we refuse to accept a fact or an experience of our reality, for example: 'I'm not a smoker; I just smoke socially' or 'I'm not upset!'. When to do with gross trauma or a disaster, denial may even be a beneficial initial response, but prolonged or habitual denial keeps us from seeing our blind spots and dealing with our issues or wounds.

Repression

This is when we simply forget about something painful or unpleasant, like when we black out during an accident. We may completely block out childhood abuse or other traumatic event from our conscious memory, or more trivially, forget to do something we dislike, like go to the dentist or do our taxes. Like denial, repression may temporarily help us cope with a traumatic experience, but in the long run it can keep us from releasing the trauma from the emotional and physical body, and prolong its negative impact on our life.

Regression

When we get triggered under stress and revert back to a childlike emotional state, responding in childlike, destructive ways, this is regression. It could be a tantrum (think road rage!), or retreating under blankets after a bad day, or giving someone the silent treatment because they have made us feel bad, mad or sad.

Displacement

This means transferring our painful emotions (that could potentially get us into trouble) from their original target to someone or something more harmless or defenseless. For example, we are mad at our boss but, instead of communicating it to him, we get home and take it out on our spouse, child or dog. Or an older child may displace their frustration from the teacher or friend to a younger sibling.

Projection

It can be a bit trickier to detect projection. It means putting our own insecurities, judgments, fears or other unpleasant feelings onto others. Here's an example: Let's say we (consciously or unconsciously) judge ourselves as stupid or fat. So we will interpret other people's words, looks or other communication as criticism of our weight or intellect, even if in their reality it is not critical at all. Or we blame other people of a behavior that we frequently engage in ourselves. 'People are so judgmental!'

Reaction formation

In short, this means expressing the opposite of our inner feelings (that we don't want to admit) in our outward behavior. For example, someone who is feeling insecure but acts over confidently or even arrogantly in order to cover it up. Or an outwardly homo-phobic person who is hiding their own hidden attraction to the same sex. Or a person who is secretly jealous of rich people but outwardly condemns their wealth instead.

Intellectualization

This means that we distance ourselves from our emotions by using the intellectual mind. That way we can maintain a cold, distant approach to the problem so that it doesn't affect us emotionally. For example focusing solely on practicalities surrounding a family member's death, serious accident or terminal illness.

Rationalization

As with intellectualization, we try to explain something away and find a logical justification to make ourselves feel better. We come up with reasons why it really wasn't that bad and why the fault was not in us but in someone else or the circumstance. For example, after being left by a partner we adored, we find faults in them to turn it into a good thing and make ourselves feel less sad.

(We Westerners have a tendency to live up in our heads, over-think and over-analyse and rely on our intellect, abandoning our feelings, which live in the body rather than head – even making them wrong.)

Sublimation

A more mature defense, sublimation is when we channel unacceptable impulses, thoughts or feelings into more acceptable ones, for example, redirecting our aggression into vigorous exercise.

There are also many roles, addictions and avoidance tactics that we use in order not to feel or own our feelings, and in order not to share our true self with others:

Keeping busy is probably the most common method of escape in our society. When we are constantly busy doing, we don't have time to be present, feel or connect with one another. Work, schedules, chores, activities, devices and entertainment fill up our day and there is little time left for connecting with ourselves and how we feel, let alone with each other.

Humor can be a defense, especially when it is constant or happens at inappropriate times, replacing compassion or other more appropriate responses.

Addictions are another widespread way of avoiding or numbing out feelings. They can be obvious ones such as alcohol, cigarettes, drugs, gambling, video games or internet porn, or less obvious but just as common like exercise, music, yoga, meditation, shopping, dieting, food, love and sex addiction, and so on. Addictions come in many different forms (substance abuse vs. process addiction), but their purpose is usually the same: to fill the void of an unmet (childhood) need, and / or to escape from or numb out the uncomfortable feelings that arise from it. (Some might argue that addictions are a brain disorder. This may be true – I am no addiction expert. But what I do see in my work is that when emotional wounds are healed, this particular type of brain disorder tends to become asymptomatic.)

Spiritual bypassing

First described by psychologist John Welwood in 1984, spiritual bypassing is a common but lesser known form of avoidance both in the modern spiritual circles as well as in strict religions. It means the use of religious or spiritual practices and beliefs in order to avoid dealing with our painful feelings, unresolved wounds, relationship issues and developmental needs. It is much more common than we realize.

Spiritual bypassing – delusions of having arrived at a higher level of being

This is what Robert Masters, PhD, says:

Spiritual bypassing is a very persistent shadow of spirituality, manifesting in many ways, often without being acknowledged as such. Aspects of spiritual bypassing include exaggerated detachment, emotional numbing and repression, overemphasis on the positive, anger-phobia, blind or overly tolerant compassion, weak or too porous boundaries, lopsided development (cognitive intelligence often being far ahead of emotional and moral intelligence), debilitating judgment about one's negativity or shadow elements, devaluation of the personal relative to the spiritual, and delusions of having arrived at a higher level of being.[27]

How to spot a defense

A defense is always there 'so that':

so that we would be

- liked
- loved
- accepted
- admired
- respected
- protected...

or so that we would not be

- judged
- abandoned
- criticized
- hurt
- made wrong
- exposed
- in pain...

or so that the other person (or people) would feel or see us or think of us a certain way.

You get the idea. In essence, many of our defenses are a form of manipulation. That is how we learnt to get our needs met as children.

The authentic self and our authentic feelings are hidden underneath all that. Until we are able to access our authentic self we stay stuck in our life and dysfunctional relationships.

PRACTICE

Next time you catch yourself acting in a certain way 'so that' (your partner would notice how you feel without telling him / her how you feel; your partner would NOT know how you really feel; someone would / wouldn't think of you a certain way…) stop!

Go deeper and investigate what it is that you really feel and desire in that moment. Particularly if it is a situation with a significant other, close friend or family member. Then communicate it directly – as scary as it is.

Real connection only takes place when we drop our defenses and allow ourselves to be vulnerable and authentic.
Liisa Halme

Uncover your (negative) core beliefs

What you believe, both consciously and unconsciously, shapes your reality.
Are unconscious beliefs sabotaging your life?

Early in life we form what are called our *core beliefs*. They are those deep-seated beliefs about the world and about ourselves that we build our whole life and personal *paradigm* (personal reality) around.

Any negative, unwanted patterns in relationships or other areas of our life are because of these beliefs that secretly run our thoughts, feelings and actions. Originally these subconscious decisions were made in order to protect us, but a lot of them simply don't work in our favor any more.

How do you know if you have negative core beliefs?

The evidence is in your external reality: your life, health, wealth, success and relationships.

If you continuously struggle in any, or all, of these areas, you can be certain that some unwanted core beliefs are running the show. They can be so ingrained that you don't see them as beliefs at all, but as absolute reality, something that 'just is'. You may think your problems are because of your partner, your genes, boss, culture, or some other external factor, but that is almost never actually the case.

You may want to object to this statement (we love blaming others, fate, something, anything). However I urge you to consider for a moment what it means: when you realize that you have been creating the problems yourself, even if unconsciously, you also hold the power to change them!

It's not a piece of cake to uncover our core beliefs as they tend to be completely hidden in the shadow part of us; that part of us which is unconscious. Consciously we may actually think something completely different, for example we may *think* that we are worthy and lovable and great, but underneath we hold a secret belief that we are not.

This will manifest in our reality through the things we attract (in other words: the things we choose) into our life, such as relationships where we feel unloved or unappreciated, jobs where we feel undervalued, or lack of success that doesn't reflect what we consciously think we deserve. Obviously this doesn't just happen magically: Our beliefs affect our reality through the choices we make and the through actions we take as a result of them. We also interpret our reality through the filter of our beliefs.

In other words, when we have repetitive patterns in our life that aren't working for us, they are usually run by negative core beliefs about ourselves or about the world. We live our lives proving these beliefs true. They *are* true for us.

For example, if I have the belief that men can't be trusted, or that it isn't safe to love romantically, I will keep proving this by finding myself in relationships where I end up betrayed or hurt in some way and I'll choose partners who prove my belief right.

Or perhaps I will make sure that I am the first one to leave, or avoid intimate relationships altogether, so that I will never end up betrayed or hurt.

Sometimes core beliefs drive you to defend yourself in ways that prove the opposite. Let me give an example: I was always the straight A student at school. I was pretty and successful in most things I set my mind to. I always strived to be the best I could (read: 'I was an obsessive perfectionist') and most of the time managed this quite well.

So it may come as a surprise when I tell you that later on in life I discovered this was all because I had a belief that there was *something wrong with me*, and that *I wasn't good enough*.

It was actually because of these beliefs that I was so driven to keep proving myself to be perfect and right, in order to keep my 'wrongness' hidden from the world and myself!

Little did I know that my success was driven by beliefs such as 'I am stupid' or 'I am less-than because I am a woman'. Ouch.

You can be sure that uncovering these was like squeezing water from a stone. After all, I was a girl from Finland, a country that is proud of its progressive equality between the sexes. And I was always proud of my intellect, and that I found school easy and got top grades with little effort.

What's wrong with being successful, driven or striving to be perfect? Nothing of course. However, when it is at the expense of how you feel inside (never good enough, ashamed of the tiniest 'imperfection', too afraid of rejection and criticism to be vulnerable or truly intimate with others…) it isn't a fulfilling way to live. In fact it is exhausting.

I ended up living through my defense, rather than my authentic self. My defense was functional and fantastic on the outside, but it left me feeling isolated, defensive, afraid and ashamed in the inside. And, by the way, fear and shame were emotions I never would have associated with myself! I just didn't 'do' them. (This is what I mean about some of our beliefs and emotions being unconscious.)

In fact fear and shame were so ingrained into my being that it took me ages to recognize them. I didn't even know what they felt like, because I had *always* felt them. They had become my normal.

The great thing is, later on, when I started to let go of some of my negative core beliefs, I still got to keep those external things that did work for me. But I no longer felt like I had to hide it if I made a mistake, or obsess over being the best and prettiest and know best in every situation (or else…).

As a result I learnt to actually love myself without so many strict conditions. I was able to be more authentically myself as a friend, partner or teacher, and it brought me a lot closer to all the important people in my life.

As we change our core beliefs, our actual reality will change along with them!

As you can tell, finding out our core beliefs is a bit like solving a mystery.

HERE'S ONE WAY TO UNCOVER YOUR CORE BELIEFS

Take a pen and paper. Think of a struggle that you have at the moment, or something that you struggle with on a regular basis. Let's say your partner works too much and is never at home, or you have a physical challenge of some kind. Write it down.

Take a moment and close your eyes and take a few, deep breaths. Let yourself drop down from your head and thoughts and into the body. Let your answers come from your subconscious – don't think about them too much. Write down the first thing that comes to mind. No answer is silly. Keep it short (the long answers tend to come from the conscious mind, but we need to go deeper than that).

Start with your struggle

He is always at work and never home.

Then:

- It makes me feel… (annoyed).
- I make it mean that… (he doesn't care about me / work is more important than me)
- This must mean that I am … (not as important as his work).
- It must be because… (he doesn't really love me).
- The reason is… (because I am not… enough).
- This must mean that I am…

Because…

– and so on.

The above scenario and answers are examples only. You'll of course come up with your own. Write down the first answer that comes to mind! Don't edit or make it sound prettier than it is. We want to get deep down and dirty!

Remember that this is about uncovering our core beliefs about *ourselves* and about the world. So 'He is a wanker' is not a core belief! Core beliefs tend to be short and simple, childish language (remember that they were formed very early on in life). So, our adult conscious mind may come up with, 'I'm not as intelligent as I should be' but the raw kid version would be 'I'm stupid'. Other common negative core beliefs are:

- I am wrong / there is something wrong with me
- I am broken
- I am bad
- I have done something wrong
- I am useless
- I am less-than because I am a woman / man
- I am alone

- The world isn't safe
- I am nothing
- I should have been a boy / girl
- It isn't safe to love.

Sounds rather full on, I know! But you can imagine what a reality built around one or more of these beliefs would look like. This is why it's helpful to uncover them, see them for what they are and let them go – and then build your reality around a new set of beliefs chosen with more consciousness.

People will do anything, no matter how absurd, in order to avoid facing their own Soul. One does not become enlightened by imagining figures of light, but by making the darkness conscious.[28]

Carl Jung

Understanding our two minds

Who wears the pants: the conscious or the unconscious mind?

How many times have you decided that you will – or will not – do something – eat more healthily or exercise more, or react in a particular way in a certain situation – only to find yourself repeating the same old pattern again despite the good intentions? Do you sometimes find that mere willpower just isn't enough?

When we want to make a specific change happen in our life, from stopping an annoying habit to something big and life altering, it is important to understand the different aspects of our our mind: the conscious and the unconscious, and how the they work together or against each other.

Conscious mind

As the name suggests, the conscious mind covers that which we are aware of: the thoughts, actions, sensations, perceptions, memories and feelings as well as things happening outside of ourselves which are within our current awareness.

But did you know that our conscious mind is only the tip of the iceberg? Underneath the surface is the much bigger part of the iceberg, the unconscious. Things that stay hidden from conscious awareness stay in the unconscious.

Unconscious mind

This consists of the primitive, instinctual and automatic responses as well as the information that we can't or don't need to consciously access. During our childhood, we accumulated countless memories and experiences that contributed to who we are today. We created beliefs and decisions about ourselves and about the world based on these experiences we can no longer recall.

These unconscious forces – beliefs, patterns, decisions, subjective maps of reality – drive our behaviors today.

The non-conscious awareness takes charge when we are operating on auto-pilot. For example, when walking home you might be on the phone with somebody, giving the conversation your conscious attention. However your unconscious mind can access the information required and lead the way home without your being alert to the path or surroundings.

There isn't *a place* called the unconscious or conscious mind. They are only metaphors. All day long our thoughts, actions and decisions ebb and flow between our conscious and non-conscious awareness.

Who's the boss?

The best analogy I have heard describes the conscious mind as the captain of a ship and the unconscious as the crew. If the captain and the crew aren't in agreement and want to go in different directions, the crew, or the unconscious mind, will almost always win. It has much more power: The conscious mind is said to be responsible for only about 10 percent of all our decision making!

So in order to get our willpower to really work and make our decisions stick, we need to get the unconscious mind on board and get clear about the hidden beliefs and motivations that might be holding us back and working against what we consciously want to achieve.

How to access the unconscious

Here's the tricky part: Since the unconscious stuff isn't available to our conscious mind, how do we access it? Unconscious material requires strong, specific triggers to surface, and we may need the assistance of a skilled professional or an honest friend to work with it. Here are some helpful tips.

Notice your emotions

A good way to begin to study your unconscious mind is to pay closer attention to your feelings and emotions. When responding or reacting to something your thinking mind often gets stuck in the story: who did or said what, your interpretation and judgements of the events.

When you pay attention to your emotions you learn a lot more. You can get in touch with what drives your reaction, be it internal or external. For example, when something happens that upsets you and you react in a certain way, instead of paying all your attention to the external factors, but noticing how you actually feel, perhaps you find that it left you feeling unloved, unappreciated or made wrong.

When you get in the habit of doing this all the time, you can notice patterns that can tell you a lot about the unconscious filters through which you interpret and experience life.

Hypnosis

In a hypnotic trance we cross the bridge between the conscious and the unconscious. It isn't anything mystical or magical; in fact we are in and out of hypnotic trance multiple times each day! A skilled hypnotherapist can use hypnosis as a vehicle to help us change negative beliefs and re-negotiate with our unconscious to re-align it with the conscious decisions in order to make significant change happen very quickly and easily.

Hypnosis and hypnotherapy can be used for anything where the mind is involved. It accelerates the effectiveness of practical or strategic psychotherapy. Hypnotherapy is particularly helpful when we want to change a specific pattern or behavior such as to stop smoking, put an end to our addiction to Ben & Jerry's cookie dough ice cream, or get over fear of heights or public speaking. It is also very effective in drug free pain management. Many top athletes use hypnosis to achieve peak performance.

Therapy and psychotherapeutic practices

This isn't just something for the deeply troubled. Everyone can benefit from good, solutions and results oriented therapy. Group therapy is particularly useful for uncovering unconscious patterns and defences as well as practicing new skills and behaviours. The group collective offers an opportunity to experiment with being vulnerable, speaking our truth, setting boundaries, listening, receiving honest feedback and asking for our needs to be met in a safe environment. Hearing others share can give us many a-ha moments. Each participant acts as a mirror that speeds up our process.

Trust your your critical faculties and inner guidance to choose a conscious therapist who walks the talk, embodies their own teachings, and with whom you feel comfortable to be yourself. However be prepared to be confronted. Our unconscious mind can put up a fight and come up with various defense mechanisms to keep itself hidden. When we get triggered we have most probably hit something important!

Meditation and deep relaxation techniques

This is another way to descend from the conscious to the unconscious for a deeper experience. Meditation or relaxation shouldn't require effort;

so choose a simple technique that doesn't involve any 'mental gymnastics'. Simple awareness of the breath and body, or use of a mantra can be helpful.

Breathwork

Our breath is the link between the sympathetic and parasympathetic nervous systems, the external and the internal world, as well as the conscious and the unconscious.

Simply put, breathwork is emotional release work (different from yogic pranayama) that uses the body's own natural release mechanisms to let go of stress, trauma and emotional build-up. It helps us access, process and heal hidden, suppressed emotional content and promotes self awareness. Look for a national breathwork association and find a listed practitioner.

The above techniques can support each other, and usually a combination works best. For example, meditation practice alone is not sufficient for the purposes of healing deep-seated emotional wounds and shouldn't be considered a replacement for high quality therapy. Likewise mere emotional releasing and catharsis without some investigation of our emotional landscape doesn't necessarily lead to deeper understanding or clarity. Neither is the understanding alone enough to give us the skills to respond more proactively or make better choices in the future.

A practical psychotherapeutic aspect needs to be included for any of these modalities to be effective as a means to heal trauma. Used skillfully they can help us get to know ourselves better, restore our sense of wholeness and function better in the world.

Good luck on your adventure into the unconscious! It is one of the most rewarding explorations you can take.

The closer you come to knowing that you alone create the world of your experience, the more vital it becomes for you to discover just who is doing the creating.[29]
Eric Micha'el Leventhal

Trusting your intuition

Learn to harness one of our most undervalued, inbuilt assets

Intuition is a very interesting form of intelligence beyond the rational mind. In our society that places a lot of emphasis on logic and reason, this part of our intelligence is often overlooked, ignored or undermined.

However we don't have to reject morals or logic in order to benefit from instinct. We can honor and use all these tools seeking balance, bringing all of the resources of our brain into action.

If only about 10-20 percent of our thinking and decision-making is conscious, that leaves 80-90 percent for non-conscious activity. So in order to maximize the use of our mental capacity and intellect, and make the best, most balanced choices for ourselves, we need to engage and give credit to the non-conscious parts of our being.

What is intuition?

The word intuition comes from the Latin *intueor,* to see; interpreted as the mind's ability to 'see' answers to problems or make decisions in the absence of logical reasoning – a 'gut reaction'.

The American psychologist and Nobel Laureate Herbert A. Simon stated that intuition is '*nothing more and nothing less than recognition*'.[30] But Albert Einstein is said to call intuition a sacred gift and the rational mind its faithful servant. My personal favourite definition is by Paramahansa Yogananda, Indian yogi and guru (known from his famous autobiography titled *Autobiography of a Yogi*). He defined intuition as '*the discriminate faculty that enables you to decide which of two lines of reasoning is right*'. He also added that '*Perfect intuition makes you master of all.*'

Today's quantum physicists such as Dr Amit Goswami (as seen in the film, *What the Bleep Do We Know*) are finding more interesting data on nature of consciousness and intuition in their studies of human universal consciousness,[31] which is shared consciousness beyond the individual brain and its personal recognition.

A common example of intuition is when you just have a gut feeling about something that may even go against your logic or reason – and it turns out to be right. Or another example, verging on telepathy, is when you just happen to think of somebody you haven't thought of for a while, perhaps even pick up the phone to call them, when it rings in your hand – and who else is on the line than the person you just thought of!

In spiritual terms intuition is also seen as the knowing through our connection to spirit. This could be yet another even more expansive form of universal consciousness.

How to engage it

Spiritual guru Deepak Chopra instructs that the best way to learn to engage intuition is by learning to '*still the mind, ask a question and feel the body*'.

Here are some other ways to get in touch with that deep internal voice and its guidance:

Journaling and writing

Without any specific intention or agenda, just let your stream of consciousness flow on paper. A good time to do this is first thing in the morning before your mind gets filled with the events of the day. The words don't need to be composed or make sense to you; just let them arise from a deeper part of you, beyond intellect.

You can also have interesting conversations between your conscious and unconscious minds in writing: the conscious mind writes with your dominant hand and the unconscious mind with the other hand. Again, don't think about it too much; just allow the words to be written on paper without trying to make sense of it then and there.

Connect to your feelings
Find a safe space where you can let yourself connect to your emotional experience and feelings, which are directly linked to intuition. Stay with the emotions in their pure form, without attaching them to the story, explanation or rational reasoning. Simply allow yourself to feel.

Trusting your gut

Did you know that we have more brains than one? The second one is referred to when we say we have a 'gut feeling' about something.

When studying intuition and our inner knowing it is helpful to understand and acknowledge this often overlooked part of the body.

Besides the cranial brain we have another significant but less studied information center, the so-called *abdominal-pelvic brain*,[32] which is a bundle or nerves located in the lower abdominal cavity and pelvis, directly connected to the autonomous nervous system. It contains more sympathetic nerves (fight / flight) than any other part of the body.

For example in a danger situation the abdominal-pelvic brain begins to sense that something is wrong and sends signals to the cranial brain and the body to be alert. If there is no evidence to support the intuitive sensations of the abdominal-pelvic brain, our logical reasoning will generally override its sensations.

However during trauma the body places priority on the abdominal-pelvic brain over the cranial brain. This is another reason why traditional talk therapy and logical analysis alone are often insufficient in releasing deep-seated trauma.

I am by no means saying we should discard logic or reason, and only go with our gut. An intelligent co-operation of both logic and intuition usually works best. Our society tends to belittle sensory experience and intuition in everyday ordinary life. However it was vital for our ancestors and is still extremely valuable for us today.

Learning to know when to trust our inner knowing and guidance is one of the most transformational steps to living our life to its full potential.

Watch the inner critic

Often the logical mind, the neocortex part of the brain, wants to rationalize away the voices of the unconscious and intuition that come from the much older so-called primitive brain that is in charge of our instincts. Try to listen to these voices without judgement and allow this inner dialogue to unfold without making it wrong.

Intuition is a very powerful thing. More powerful than intellect, in my opinion.[33]
Steve Jobs

How to relax a busy mind

'Just relax' is often easier said than done. Here's what to do when your mind goes on overdrive.

Even in moments when everything else is quiet, the lights are out and the TV, smart phones and all noise is off, the inside of our mind can still be a very busy place. It is the one place we cannot escape, even if we do try to distract or suppress it in so many different ways: by constant doing, drinking, drugs and partying, adrenaline addiction, over-exercising, over-shopping, over-eating – you name it. When our persistent mental activity becomes exhausting and disturbs our ability relax and sleep, it's definitely time to do something about it.

You've probably heard that meditation is a way to quieten the mind, but let's face it, if your mind is constantly racing, it can be pretty hard to meditate! The ancient yogis knew this and developed the physical practice including the asanas – the yoga postures – and breathing practices to prepare the body and mind for meditation.

Even if yoga isn't your thing a lot can be learnt from this approach.

Get out of your mind and into your body

Some of our common forms of self-medication are more or less on the right track.

What helps us get out of the mind is getting into the body! Doing things that encourage us to become aware of the physical body and its sensations, the breath, and so on, can be very meditative.

This is a very different kind of body awareness than the self-conscious critical study we do in front of the mirror: it involves feeling and being aware of the body from the inside, noticing all the physical sensations, tensions and energies. Activities that guide your awareness into the body and breath could be tai chi, qi gung, martial arts, dance, surfing, yoga, running, singing and breathwork, just to name a few.

The activity doesn't need to be anything draining. Over-exercising is a way to numb ourselves out by exhaustion, but it doesn't necessarily help to relax the mind in the long term.

Get in the zone

One of the steps leading to quieting the mind – and meditation – is relaxed concentration. When the mind is focused on something we love, it becomes completely absorbed with that one thing, undistracted by worries or other thoughts.

Hence it is valuable to find what you love doing, and do it! Whether it is playing the guitar, gardening, painting, snowboarding, golf, dancing, listening to classical music… just make sure you create yourself plenty of time for it regularly. Let yourself get 'in the zone'. In these states of natural flow we descend from higher frequency gamma and beta brainwaves states associated with alertness, anxiety and fight-or-flight to lower alpha wavelengths and experience more relaxation, easy learning, light trance states and increased serotonin ('feel-good' hormone) production.

The more we get used to dropping into and staying in alpha state, the more easily we will descend to theta and delta states of dreaming / REM sleep and deep sleep.

What about video games, internet and TV?

Yes, they have become so popular for the very same reason: they take our mind off the other, stressful stuff.

However studies show that staring at a screen for extended periods of time actually activates and tires the brain and nervous system more through excessive stimulus and by creating more disturbance rather than inducing relaxation response.

Sleep experts recommend taking at least an hour or two off screen devices before bedtime to allow our nervous system to relax and improve quality of our sleep.

Getting in touch with our emotions

When you listen to the mental commentary and chatter that goes on in your head you'll notice that a lot of the thoughts have an emotional charge behind them. Perhaps they are driven by fear, stress and worry; maybe they are annoyed, frustrated thoughts or angry thoughts; thoughts that make something or someone wrong; sad thoughts, ashamed or embarrassed thoughts; guilty thoughts.

Instead of getting too caught up with the content or the story (Who said or did what / What happened / What you made it mean) pay attention to the emotional energy behind the thoughts. Once you recognize the emotion, just allow yourself to feel it:

• Where do you feel it in your body?

• What does it feel like?

• What's the physical sensation?

When we have stuck emotional energies stored up in our body they keep producing thoughts charged with that energy and cluttering the mind until we release it from our system. You can read more about emotional energies, how to identify, process and release them in Part 1 of this book!

Brainwave entertainment

There is a wide variety of brainwave entertainment on the market today that can help us descend from the mentally active states to deeper states of relaxation and meditation quickly and easily by rhythmic sounds that create an electric charge response in the brain. The brain responds to this sensory stimulation by synchronizing its own electric cycles to the same rhythm.

Brainwave entertainment is the meditation of the techno age!

Whatever method of meditation or relaxation you apply in your own life, the space and stillness you create in your mind is peace of the deepest kind. If you want to create harmony and calm in your life and the world, then your own head is the best place to start!

Tension is who you think you should be. Relaxation is who you are.
Chinese proverb

What's really holding you back?

Identifying your unconscious beliefs, thoughts and emotions that keep you stuck.

If you could be doing anything you want in your life, what would you do? What would your lifestyle be like? Where and how would you live? Take a moment to daydream, let yourself doze off into a reverie about what your life would be like in this alternative, or shall we say potential, reality.

In the pursuit of the life you dream of, it is worthwhile to look at what is actually holding you back from having all that you desire.

A lot of the time the things we *think* are holding us back – lack of money, talent or resources, our age or health, responsibilities or other apparent things – are actually indicators of something deeper: the unconscious negative beliefs that shape our reality and keep it within the limits of what we think possible. These beliefs can make us overlook our potential and forget that we always have a choice. They keep us small and make us settle for less.

I'll never forget an elderly lady who visited the safari camp where I used to work in a remote jungle in Tanzania, East Africa. To get there you had to fly a bush plane from a major airport, land on a little air strip that was nothing more than a patch of grass populated by cows and goats, then take a small dinghy to the bigger dhow boat, ride a couple of hours on the dhow in the clear waters of Lake Tanganyika, and finally get to the sandy shore on the dinghy again. The main attraction in Mahale was a group of wild chimpanzees, and to see them usually meant hours of strenuous hiking in the jungle. This silver-haired lady, Rose, who was in her seventies, had severe MS (multiple sclerosis). She couldn't walk without help. Even then it was tediously slow and she needed to rest after a few minutes. Rose couldn't use her wheelchair because there were no footpaths or roads around. She had to be helped with pretty much everything, and she accepted the help gracefully. She ventured out to the jungle to see the chimpanzees on a special chair the guys at the camp had made for her. A strong man carried her at each end, just like in old movies. Rose also joined us on a snorkeling trip (picture the transitions from the dinghy to the dhow, then to the water almost 2 meters down, then back on the dhow and the dinghy again...) to see the bright colored fish. This amazing woman let nothing stop her. Nothing was too hard, or too much of an effort. Everybody was happy to help her and there were many able bodied people around to assist, literally carrying her on and off boats and over the soft sand. The place was as far from wheelchair friendly as it gets. Did I mention Rose had flown there all the way from New Zealand!

Personal success

What makes extraordinary or successful people different from others is not necessarily their outstanding IQ, their incredible luck, the family or circumstance they were born into or the amount of work they have put in – although some of the above can be contributing factors.

What is different about successful people is that they believe in themselves and believe it's worth going for what they desire. Whatever they want, they make it happen.

What we are talking about here is personal success: living the life we want to be living regardless of whether our dreams are big or small in the eyes of other people. Living our dream could be running a small flower shop at a train station or being a famous musician or a CEO of a large company – or perhaps a very fulfilled mother / father of four, looking after kids at home, cooking with love for our friends and family.

Personal success isn't so much about what it looks like on the outside, but more about what it *feels* like on the inside: happy, fulfilled, inspired, passionate.

Going back to the little daydream… now ask yourself:

• What is in the way?
• Why isn't this the reality you currently live?
• Why is it not possible?

Take a pen and paper and actually write the reasons down.

What did you write?

The first answers will sound more logical and sense-making. However underneath these sensible answers will be deeper hidden reasons.

You can continue each sentence or reason deeper and deeper following this format:

• The reason I don't have X is because…
• and that must be because…
• which is because…

Write without thinking about it too much. The answers don't need to make sense. Don't start analyzing or reasoning, just write the first thing that comes to mind.

The suppressed and unconscious emotions such as fear, shame and guilt go hand in hand with the negative beliefs that hold us back.

• Do you fear failing?
• Perhaps you are afraid of having what you want and then losing it?
• What about the reactions of others if you were to succeed?

- Is yours a fear of committing yourself to your dream because you may feel guilty about being happy when there are many so miserable?
- Would you feel ashamed or guilty to have more than others?

The downsides

Another way to uncover your unconscious beliefs and emotions is to close your eyes and imagine already having the life you desire, in all its glory: having already lost the weight, published the novel, reached the success, having the relationship of your dreams or whatever it is your heart desires.

Then have a look at the disadvantages of having it all:

- Would your friends be jealous of you?
- Would people try to put you down?
- Would you be uncomfortable with the fame and success?
- Would you feel safe being in your dream body and having more attention from the opposite sex?

These downsides will reveal your *fears* around having what you want. It's good to remember they are just fears, and can be worked with.

Your reality reflects your beliefs

If you are still not sure what your personal hang-ups are, look at recurring themes in your life and relationships. Your external reality and circumstance are largely a reflection of your inner reality. Why? Because your thoughts, beliefs and emotions drove the choices and actions that took you where you are today. You can imagine how beliefs like 'I'm not good at…' or 'you can't earn a living with…' might influence the choices you make. Or how 'it's all too hard' or 'I already know that' kind of attitudes prevent you from learning the necessary skills and taking the steps to create the life you want.

If you have the belief that you are not good enough you will find plenty of proof to back it up, maybe never quite reaching the standards you set for yourself. Or you project onto others and find that *other people* or the world never quite live up to your expectations, as a reflection and a cover-up of your own 'not good enough' story.

Two common things that trip us up are 1) what you don't know that you don't know, and 2) what you think you know but isn't so.

Bringing our limiting beliefs into awareness and seeing them for what they are – a fabrication – frees us from their grip. Then we can open the door for other possibilities, and start changing dysfunctional or unhelpful beliefs for better ones that lead us to take positive action towards our dreams.

When we are unconscious, we feel stuck. When we become conscious, we remember our freedom to choose.
Liisa Halme

You are more powerful than you think

How your thoughts, feelings and beliefs affect the reality you create for yourself.

Science tells us that everything in us and around us consists of an energy vibration, a frequency. As a concept it is nothing new. However the consequences are somewhat revolutionary: it means that when we alter the energy frequency, the structure of the physical matter changes.

Our emotions, thoughts and beliefs alike are energy frequencies; creators of that reality. Quantum physics now shows what the yogis and many ancient philosophers have known for centuries – that reality is relative, and actually composed by the expectation of the observer. We literally manifest what we believe in, whether we are aware of it or not.

Placebo – is it 'just' in the mind?

One example of this is the placebo effect. A placebo is an inactive medical treatment such as saline solution or a starch tablet. Around one third of people who take placebos experience measurable, observable, or felt improvement in health or behavior, or an end to their symptoms. This is called the placebo effect. It is shown in all medical trials and studies that about 30 percent or more of *all* drug effects are placebo effects: something independent of the of the drug itself. This is huge!

The placebo effect is just one known and scientifically recognized example of how incredibly powerful the mind is, and that whatever we believe in shapes our physical reality.

If 30 percent of people find improvement to their health and symptoms merely by taking a fake medication, imagine what we could change if we learnt to intelligently harness this incredible power within us, the power of faith.

This is why we should pay attention to our belief systems, particularly the ones we take for granted: the more attached to our beliefs we are, the more they shape our reality. We find more and more evidence to back up our beliefs, regardless of whether we have chosen them consciously or absorbed them unconsciously.

When we are influenced and programmed by somebody else, such as our families, culture and society, then our reality becomes theirs; not ours.

The shadow side of our power

Since we are only aware of a fraction of our thoughts, feelings and decisions, the vast majority of our experience that shapes our world is hidden and unconscious.

Uncovering those hidden parts of our mind and experience is the way to becoming more conscious and making more mindful choices for ourselves. Fear, for example, is a very slow, dense vibration of energy. It brings us into a very heavy, dense, slow vibrating state.

I, for example, had this unconscious belief that it was not safe to be a woman and that 'I am less-than because I am a woman'. Hence I was very much in my male energy well into my early thirties, forsaking my femininity as something inferior (although I did use my sexual energy and sexuality as a power – but that's another story).

I always related better with men or more masculine women. I had a very boyish body and had never had a natural menstrual cycle. Because of this, according to many doctors over the years, I would not be able to conceive or have children naturally.

Once I uncovered these hidden beliefs and worked on letting them go, embraced my feminine essence and finally owned my womanhood, my physical reality changed with it. My natural cycle started, for the first time, in my thirties! About a year later I conceived our first child completely naturally, became a mother, and as I am writing this I am expecting our second child. This is how dramatically our beliefs can and do shape our physical reality!

Physics and consciousness

Over times physicists, including Albert Einstein, have assured us that the solidity of matter is a mirage. The universe is an infinite matrix of information that includes the illusory reality we believe in. This is well aligned with the wisdom of the yogis and Vedic philosophers who call our relative reality *maya*, 'the illusion'.

This also means that we have the freedom to choose the reality we believe in and create for ourselves.

Consciousness is the programming language of the universe, and we are consciousness conductors.

The more conscious we become, the more our world expands and the more aware we become of the possibilities, realizing that the perceived limitations were only beliefs that held us back in life and kept us from expressing ourselves in our full magnificence!

All matter originates and exists only by virtue of a force which brings the particle of an atom to vibration and holds this most minute solar system of the atom together. We must assume behind this force the existence of a conscious and intelligent mind. This mind is the matrix of all matter.[34]

Max Planck (Nobel Prize-winning physicist and the founder of quantum theory)

The art of manifestation

Easy steps to turning your dreams into reality

I always knew I could make my dreams come true. However I didn't always know how it actually happened. Sometimes things just came to me in the most peculiar ways. Unfortunately it also seemed that both my dreams *and* my biggest fears alike would manifest.

When I learnt more about manifestation and how it works (beyond the popular Law of Attraction, 'think of something and it will happen') it all began to make sense and I put the theory into action, tested it out and was stunned by the immediate results time and time again.

I am going to share with you what I learnt and how powerfully that can change the way you make things happen in your life: through relentless hours, days and years of hard work – or by applying the below principles and letting things *come to you* with ease and flow through perfect opportunities, so-called coincidences, without major struggle.

The doing

This is the obvious part; the effort that we need to put in. In order to make things happen in our life, whether it is getting a new job / more clients or losing weight, we have to take action towards it: learn new skills, fill out job applications, go to interviews, market ourselves, make healthier food choices and so on.

The funny thing is, when we are focusing on the *doing* and the *actions*, we sometimes get fixed on the result coming directly from those actions and can miss opportunities coming from elsewhere.

Let me explain: in promoting my business and putting energy into marketing, I may find that I get new clients, but not from the avenue where I did my marketing. Just the fact that I was putting energy into my business was generating more clients, even if they came from a completely different direction. I may have found this particular method of marketing ineffective, but in reality I was still getting results, just not in the way I expected! (The universe doesn't know the difference.)

This is not to say that you shouldn't be strategic about your business or test what actually works, but, by simply directing thought and energy into what you want, you are getting closer to it.

Or you might apply for a bunch of positions, yet the dream job ends up coming to you from an unexpected source.

So when *doing*, stay open to all other things that come your way!

It is important to note that we do need to take action towards the things we desire in life. It is not sufficient to just sit and wait for things to come to us by mere power of thought. (That is called wishing, and wishing isn't actually the most powerful form of thought.)

As essential a part as the doing is in the process; it is not the only one. We can get there by just working really hard, but there are other aspects that make manifestation a whole lot easier…

The being

This part is hugely important yet often forgotten in the manifestation process! Think of the things you want in your life or what you want to achieve or manifest. Then think of the kind of person who would have that or be that. What are they like? How would they think? What would their integrity be like? How would they speak / walk / act / dress?

Instead of waiting until you have achieved being that person, you can accelerate the process by becoming that person first and you will get there much more quickly!

If you want to attract your ideal partner, be the person that they would fall in love with. Be the kind of person who would run a successful international business, or be a successful writer or whatever reality it is you desire.

Remember it is not about pretending. It is about deeply embodying those qualities in yourself and your life.

An example

I have a friend, let's call him Ryan, who is an all-round perfect 'catch'. But he acts and behaves like the eternal bachelor that he is, and wonders why he can't find the kind of woman he could see himself committing to long term in a loving relationship. (Because that kind of woman will run a mile when she sees him!)

He is not *being* the man that attracts a life partner and a committed intimate relationship, but the naughty playboy who mostly attracts party girls looking for a short-term good time.

The feeling

Think of that thing that you really want, or what you want your life to be like. Close your eyes and let yourself imagine *you already have it*. How does it make you feel? Allow yourself those feelings to rush through your body, and write them down. What were they?

Emotion is energy, and in the process of manifestation, energy plays a hugely significant role. By growing those same emotions in your system every day by visualizing you already have that which you desire, you are filling your energy field with them, attracting more of those same energies into your life.

Here's the fun part: besides imagining and visualizing, you can also do this through other activities that give you the same feelings. Let's say having your dream made you feel freedom, joy, passion, excitement and satisfaction. Perhaps you are a surfer and being out on the waves gives you the same feelings, or maybe you love horse-riding or painting – whatever it is that brings up those same feelings in you – do more of it!

The remembering

This is an advanced visualization trick: imagine already having reached your dream. Then look back in time to see what it took for you to get there: what decision and actions led to your success. Sometimes it is easier to see the steps through remembering and looking back than trying to see the way forward into the unknown.

The speaking

When we always speak our truth, our words and thoughts become incredibly powerful. Likewise, the less truthful we are, both with ourselves and with each other, the less power our words and thoughts have.

Do you think you are always truthful?

Let me ask you a few questions!

- Do you sometimes say yes when really you want to say no?
- Do you at times pretend to listen to someone when really your mind is elsewhere?
- Do you ever say nice things you don't really mean, just to be polite?
- How often do you tell yourself or your partner you are going to do something, but don't?
- Do you sometimes say 'It's okay' when actually it's not quite?

Pay attention to where you are not being as truthful as you could be, and watch your word – and yourself – become more and more powerful every day!

Another way you may be sabotaging your dreams with your words is by putting yourself down. Do you minimize what you desire in life or avoid speaking about it at all? Do you find it hard to accept compliments or find a way to dodge them? You may think you are being humble but you could actually be denying yourself what you desire.

It is perfectly possible to accept a compliment in a humble way (just say 'Thank you; that's nice to hear', for example).

Thought + emotion + inspired action = dream manifested

PRACTICE TO MANIFEST A NEW REALITY

Take this as a fantasy play! Let yourself relax and close your eyes. You can play some pleasant, relaxing music (preferably instrumental) to help you drop into a dream-like alpha state. Let your breathing slow down and deepen.

Imagine a situation that you would like to see change in your life: Maybe it's a more fulfilling relationship, a healthier body, or finishing the book you want to write – whatever you desire.

Instead of worrying about how to get there and the obstacles on the way, imagine it's already happened: you have what you desire! How do you feel? How do you breathe? How do you hold yourself? What are the emotions you feel? Let these emotions grow bigger in your body; take time to actually *feel* them!

What has changed in you (if anything)? How do you think differently? What kind of actions do you take? Come back to the feeling again. Let yourself feel it all: the fulfillment, the passion, the peace, the confidence, the joy, the freedom – whatever it is that it brings you.

Be aware of any unpleasant feelings as well so that you can work on them later. Are people jealous of you? Note them, and come back to the pleasant feelings.

Then make a commitment to do one thing every day that brings you some of those same pleasurable, positive feelings. It doesn't have to be related to the original dream. For example, if your dream was to take the leap and change your career, and it would make you feel more fulfillment, freedom, passion and joy, and you feel those same feelings when you surf or play guitar, then do that!

This is a way you can actually change your frequency to match that which you desire.

You and your reality are ONE. When YOU change, everything changes.[35]
Gordana Biernat

From stress to bliss

Stress response vs. relaxation response

Stress seems to be the epidemic of the century in our Western world. The estimate is that at least 75 percent, but more likely up to 90 percent, of our illness is either induced or, at the very least, exacerbated by stress.

Where short-term stress is normal and healthy and can make us perform better, prolonged stress is not our friend. Hence it is useful to have basic understanding of how stress works, its different stages, and most importantly how to release it and allow our system to return to a relaxed state on a regular basis.

What is stress and where does it come from?

We tend to think that stress comes from somewhere outside of us: pressure at work, relationship issues, financial troubles or stressful events such as accidents, illness or moving house. However stress itself is an internal physical response which evolved as a survival mechanism: the *fight-or-flight* (or adrenaline) response.

When encountering a life-threatening situation our sympathetic nervous system is activated and a surge of stress hormones prepares us to fight or to flee. As a result, our heart pounds, our muscles tense, our blood vessels constrict and we are suddenly on high alert, ready to fight or flee from a stressful or dangerous situation. Blood and energy flows from the internal organs to the extremities such as hands and feet.

However, because we already have excess stress hormones in our body, we tend to activate the fight-or-flight response multiple times during a typical day, mostly because of situations that are inconvenient but not even close to life threatening. Traffic jams, long to-do lists or work deadlines are more likely what we would face.

In other words we get excessively stressed out over relatively small things, or our stress hormone levels stay high continuously so that we don't even notice it any more. It becomes our normal. Over time, such chronic stress takes its toll on the physical body: when high levels of stress hormones are secreted often, they can contribute to a number of medical conditions such as high blood pressure, gastro-intestinal diseases, muscle tension, adrenal fatigue, anxiety disorders and much more.

The other side of stress

The more extreme and lesser-known version of stress is *the freeze* (or opiate) response. This happens after prolonged fight-or-flight response, or in an overwhelming, traumatic situation where our body and nervous system switches to a different approach; to 'playing dead'.

In the freeze state we experience stress-induced analgesia (thanks to the natural opioids), and are no longer aware of how we feel or how stressed we are. We may seem completely calm and relaxed on the outside, but we feel somewhat disconnected and dissociated. Underneath the seemingly calm surface the nervous system is still producing the stress hormones and full effects of the fight-or-flight – keeping us ready to flee as soon as the predator looks or moves away, or the immediate danger eases off.

In freeze state we dissociate from the stress and pain in order to survive (going unconscious in an accident for example). The freeze response serves its purpose in both animal and human kingdoms: Predators aren't interested in already dead prey, and in a situation where we have no chance of fighting back or fleeing successfully, our chances of survival are greater if we give up trying and simply comply. Staying stuck in prolonged, chronic freeze response can lead to multiple physical, mental and emotional health issues including depression.

Both the fight or flight and freeze responses are normal states, as long as we have the opportunity to release the stress from the system and return to baseline: our normal calm, relaxed and engaged state. The human and animal bodies naturally know how to do this through innate release mechanisms such as different breathing patterns and shaking or tremor.

However we learn to suppress these release mechanisms as we grow up, mainly because we don't want others to see how we are feeling, and as a result the stress often stays in the body and becomes chronic.

The body's own natural chill-pill

The human body, infinitely wise as it is, of course has something in its natural drug store to counter-balance the stress response.

The relaxation response, otherwise known as 'rest and digest' mode, is induced by the other side of our nervous system – the parasympathetic nervous system. It turns off fight or flight response and brings the body back to a physical state of deep relaxation, reducing stress hormone levels back to neutral and releasing other hormones such as endorphins (the body's natural pain killers) and oxytocin (the 'love hormone') into the system. It is where all our body's natural repair, regeneration, digestion and healing takes place.

The relaxation response counteracts the physiological and psychological effects of stress and may help counteract the toxic effects of chronic stress by slowing breathing rate, relaxing muscles, and reducing blood pressure, helping any health problem that is caused or exacerbated by chronic stress (the 90 percent of all illness).

Of course as we feel better again and no longer operate on survival mode, we feel more at ease in all situations; at work, socially, and in our relationships. Small things don't stress us out as much any more and we are more open to opportunities that come our way.

There are many ways to evoke the relaxation response. Here are some:

- *Visualization and deep relaxation* – try a few different techniques, either with audio or on your own.
- *Massage* – book in for a nurturing and relaxing massage (Oh dear, if I must!)
- *Acupuncture, acupressure and tapping* can help your whole nervous system calm down instantly through specific meridian points.
- *Breathe* the stress out: different breathing techniques, which you learn in a yoga class or with a breathwork practitioner, directly and immediately affect the whole nervous system.
- *Prayer and meditation* calm busy mind and elevate the soul!
- *Tai chi, qi gong and yoga* – all brilliant ancient practices. Even the biggest stress-heads walk out of a yoga class blissed out like they're on valium.
- *Mindfulness* is a combination of non-judgemental self-awareness and being present in the here and now. It takes our attention from worries about the past or future to this moment and our thoughts and feelings.
- *Stroke a furry pet* – it is proven to lower heart rate and blood pressure. It's hard to stay stressed out while cuddling a dog or a cat!

- *Kiss, cuddle and make love* – last but definitely not least. Human touch is a major stress reliever. The more pleasure, the more dopamine and oxytocin.

Learning to induce the relaxation response helps us to be better equipped to deal with life's unexpected stressors, achieve better health, easier relationships and generally feel better. Practicing just once or twice daily for 10 to 20 minutes can be enough to counteract the stress response and bring about deep relaxation and inner peace.

I'm too blessed to be stressed.
Unknown Rasta man, Barbados

De-mystifying meditation

How and why to meditate

I'm sure you've heard before that meditation is good for you, but so are many other things that we know about yet still don't necessarily apply or practice in our own lives. So what makes meditation such a special skill that we simply can't afford to miss?

My quest is to give answers to some of the most common questions and reservations about meditation and give you an easy practice to follow anywhere, anytime in those spare moments you would otherwise spend browsing on your smartphone, checking emails for the hundredth time or reading today's posts on Facebook.

What is meditation?

In short, meditation is an all-natural way to effectively reduce stress and its undesirable side effects. It induces a deep state of relaxation and a tranquil mind, clearing away built-up information overload that contributes to stress.

Yogis and advanced meditators use it to reach higher states of consciousness – but luckily you don't need to be an abstinent yogi living in a cave in order to benefit from meditation practice.

What are the benefits?

Because of its countless, scientifically proven, physical health benefits, meditation is frequently recommended by medical doctors to help with various health complaints.

Its blood pressure lowering effect helps people with heart problems and high blood pressure. The reduction in tension-related pain provides relief for headaches, ulcers, muscle and joint problems and chronic pain. Increased production of neurotransmitters and such as serotonin (the 'happy neurotransmitter') and endorphins (the 'natural high neurotransmitters') and lowered stress hormone levels assist in overcoming depression and anxiety, help us sleep, digest and generally feel better.

Overall immune system function is improved and fatigue reduced.

Many meditation experts claim that 20 minutes of meditation equals about two hours of deep sleep.

The effects on our emotional well-being are also significant: meditation can help us gain new perspective in stressful situations and improve our skills in managing them. Our self-awareness is improved, we become more attentive and able to focus on the present moment. Meditation also helps to release negative emotions.

Keep it simple

We can use different meditation techniques, according to preference, to induce and evoke that stillness of the mind, but essentially meditation happens, without our *trying to do* anything! Regardless of the brand or style of meditation you go for, I recommend to keep it simple.

Meditation does not involve mental or physical effort – and this is where we can get it wrong, turning it into some kind of 'mental acrobatics'.

Sri Krishnamacharya, the teacher of those yogis and teachers who brought yoga into the West, used to say: '*You cannot meditate! Meditation arises as a gift, as a siddhi, when the circumstance is right*' – such as, after a yoga practice or when looking at the ocean or listening to the rain.

What you need

Meditation practice is simple and inexpensive, doesn't require any special equipment. You can start with a course, or just learn by yourself – it's easy!

In the beginning it is helpful to find a quiet place, although once you're used to it you can meditate anywhere, anytime, even on a busy bus or train or a waiting room. For now, choose a place where you can sit comfortably and away from disturbances for a few minutes. Turn your phone off.

HOW TO MEDITATE

Find a relaxed sitting position either on a chair, or on the floor on a cushion if you are comfortable sitting cross-legged. I recommend having your back supported so that you can sit with the spine upright without effort or strain.

Close your eyes and rest your hands in your lap or on your thighs. Take a couple of deep relaxed breaths, letting all the air out on the exhale, using the out-breath to relax the whole body.

Let your awareness move from your head and thoughts and the things outside of you, down into your body and breath. Resume a normal natural breathing rhythm and let the air flow freely in and out without any effort. Simply notice your breath without trying to change or analyse it in any way. Notice the body responding to the inhale and the exhale.

Simply keep following your breath in and out. Each time you notice your mind wandering and beginning to think again, gently guide your attention and awareness back to the breath. This will help your mind to reduce its level of activity and evoke the relaxation response in your nervous system.

Thoughts will come and go like clouds in the sky. Just let them come and let them go without engaging with them. Gaps will start to appear between thoughts, and with time they will get longer. But the nature of the mind is to think, so it's no use trying not to! Thoughts or no thoughts, it's all okay.

Mantra

If you want, you can internally repeat a simple mantra, such as 'let' on the inhale and 'go' on the exhale. If you choose to use a mantra it is a good idea to use the same one each time: the mantra will help you focus and quieten your mind and also work as an anchor that your nervous system learns to associate with the deep relaxation.

Next time you use the mantra it will take you back into that deep state more quickly! Your mind will take the sound of the words to play with – much like a catchy song that plays back in your head again and again without any trying.

You can start with as little as five to ten minutes, and progress to meditating 20-30 minutes at a time, perhaps even twice a day. You might want to start your day with meditation or do it at lunchtime or after work. It's totally up to you.

The main thing is to find a time that works within your life. You could make a habit of meditating during your bus or train commute to work, while you breastfeed your baby or first thing in the morning before you actually get up. If you normally find it hard to switch off after work it might be a good time to meditate so that you can be more present in your personal life.

It's better to meditate a short time every day than an hour once a week.

Most importantly, relax and enjoy – don't make meditation another thing to achieve or stress about!

You should sit in meditation 20 minutes every day, unless you are too busy – then you should sit for an hour.
Old Zen saying

Let's wrap it up

I hope these chapters give you the tools to set yourself free! Remember that it isn't enough to just read and understand the concepts, but they are something to continue practicing and embodying in your daily life. Through deep inner work you will you experience the newfound freedom that I speak of!

Note that this is all for the purposes of your *personal* inner work and these principles are for you to choose (or not) to practice, not something to impose on anyone or use as some kind of moral or spiritual high ground. They are also not principles to repeat like a pseudo-intellectual parrot without deeper understanding or embodiment, but ones to practice and apply to your own life. They are not tools for avoiding intimacy or the inevitable disarray of life, but tools for deepening intimacy with it all.

There are no *shoulds* here. There is nothing to believe in or agree with; only to test, experience and decide for yourself.

It is completely normal to encounter inner resistance to these ideas – after all you have constructed and believed in a certain kind of reality your whole life – so the thought of changing it can be scary and confronting. It may be challenging to change your paradigm and let go of old beliefs because you like to be right and it would be like admitting you were wrong all along. You may even feel protective of your struggle and justify it in very credible ways, backing it up with medical, circumstantial or other evidence. Of course you have all the right in the world to do this; to reject all that you've read here and keep living the way you have. But if you have read this book, my guess is that you are seeking some kind of a change.

This is the change you crave for! Now you can sit in the driver's seat of your life and live fully, not be blindly driven by the unconscious parts of you. After all you've got nothing to lose: If it doesn't work then you can always go back to your old way of life.

More and more you'll notice how all of these different things tie in together and how they makes sense together as a whole. You will realize your role as the active creator of your life and your experience. The more you get to know yourself and reclaim your personal power by taking responsibility of your life, including your health, success and relationships, the less you feel the need to try to control things you ultimately cannot control – other people, for example. You will also find that you'll feel more at ease with what is, at ease with yourself and with the world; and you'll feel free to just LIVE – live your purpose and your passion while being authentically you.

I would love to hear from you, of your successes and struggles. Please stay in touch and connect with me on: www.liisahalme.com

The not-so-small small print:

Please beware that any of these topics and principles can be taken to the extreme, taken out of context and misused. Everything in this book is for you judge, consider and evaluate for yourself, and if you so wish, to experiment with and adapt to your own life situations. It is by no means intended as the Ultimate Truth, but rather as something that worked for me (and many many others), that can work for you too when the going gets tough! Pain in life is a given, but suffering is optional. This book is intended to help ease your suffering and remind you that you always have a choice.

I am no prophet, and even if I were, I would advise you always to make your own judgements and decisions.

Resources

1 https://www.inc.com/marcel-schwantes/57-emotional-intelligence-quotes-to-drive-your-success.html

2 Candace Pert, Molecules of Emotion: The science behind body-mind medicine

3 https://www.biodynamicbreath.com/wp-content/uploads/2016/08/Breathwork-An-Additional-TX.pdf

4 Carl Jung, Memories Dreams and Reflections, Page 247

5 https://en.wikipedia.org/wiki/Serenity_Prayer

6 Friedrich Nietzsche, Twilight of the Idols

7 Carl Jung, Letters Vol.1, Pages 236-237

8 https://isha.sadhguru.org/global/en/wisdom/sadhguru-spot/time-for-truth

9 https://www.goodreads.com/author/quotes/568916.T_K_V_Desikachar

10 Brené Brown, The gifts of Imperfection: Let Go of Who You Think You're Supposed to Be and Embrace Who You Are

11 https://www.psychologytoday.com/blog/moral-landscapes/201112/dangers-crying-it-out AND https://www.psychologytoday.com/blog/moral-landscapes/201407/parents-misled-cry-it-out-sleep-training-reports and the research study references of each article

12 Matthew 7:7, NIV

13 Deborah Day, BE HAPPY NOW

14 Brené Brown, The gifts of Imperfection: Let Go of Who You Think You're Supposed to Be and Embrace Who You Are

15 Fyodor Dostoyevsky, 'Critical Articles' Complete Collected Works

16 Melody Beattie, Codependent No More: How to Stop Controlling Others and Start Caring for Yourself

17 Audre_Lorde, Our Dead Behind Us: Poems

18 Mark 12:31 NIV

19 Gary Chapman, The Five Love Languages: How to Express Heartfelt Commitment to Your Mate

20 Matthew 7:7, ESV

21 Matthew 7:7, ESV

22 https://www.brainyquote.com/search_results?q=martha+beck%2C+inner+child

23 Richard Bach, The Bridge Across Forever

24 https://www.goodreads.com/quotes/8237774-we-seldom-learn-much-from-someone-with-whom-we-agree

25 https://www.azquotes.com/author/2833-Pema_Chodron/tag/feelings

26 https://en.wikipedia.org/wiki/Character_structure and https://energeticsinstitute.com.au/psychotherapy-counselling/characterology/

27 http://robertmasters.com/writings/spiritual-bypassing

28 Carl Jung, Psychology and Alchemy, Page 99

29 https://www.goodreads.com/quotes/895238-the-closer-you-come-to-knowing-that-you-alone-create

30 https://www.goodreads.com/quotes/1271835-the-situation-has-provided-a-cue-this-cue-has-given

31 https://en.wikipedia.org/wiki/Universal_mind

32 Byron Robinson, The Abdominal and Pelvic Brain

33 https://www.nytimes.com/2011/10/30/opinion/sunday/steve-jobss-genius.html

34 https://en.wikiquote.org/wiki/Max_Planck

35 Gordana Biernat, *Know the Truth: Why Knowing Who You Are Changes Everything*

Printed in the United States
By Bookmasters